QUILTING

£1

5/21

Sampler wall hanging

QUILTING

CAROLINE GREEN

WARD LOCK

Copyright © 1986 Ward Lock Limited, England

First published in 1986 by
Ward Lock, Villiers House,
41/47 Strand. London WC2N 5JE

First paperback edition 1990

A Cassell imprint.

Designed by Niki fforde
Drawings by Pam Corfield
Photography by Tom Mannion
Text set in Bodoni
Printed and bound in Spain by Graficas Reunidas

ISBN 0 7063-6914-9

CONTENTS

PART I

1 TYPES OF QUILTING

Quilting can be divided into twelve separate techniques which are explained in full in this chapter. You can use just one technique on a piece of work or you can use two or three to achieve a great richness in design and decoration. In the first project (page 33), I explain how to make up a sample square of each technique which can then be stitched together to make a sampler wall hanging. This will give you a feel for all the different sorts of quilting and you can then choose your favourites for future projects of your own.

ENGLISH OR WADDED QUILTING

This quilting consists of a layer of plain top fabric, then wadding and finally a backing fabric. The traditional patterns were marked round templates and household articles such as plates, cups and wine glasses using the scratch method (page 21) on the top layer. They were then hand stitched, using a running stitch or backstitch, in a similar-coloured thread. Nowadays, we can also use machine stitch either straight or zig-zag depending on the complexity of the design and the effect you want to create.

For the traditional method, the hand stitching is best done on a frame, but small pieces can be worked in the hand without stretching. Tack your three layers together, using the frame as described on page 22. Then mark small areas of your design onto the top layer using the templates and the scratch method described on page 21. If this marking method is not suitable, choose another technique and transfer the whole design onto the fabric, before tacking the layers together. Hand stitch from the centre of the work outwards, to keep the layers even. Choose plain pale colours and matching or slightly contrasting threads for this traditional look. Silks, cottons, lawn, wool/cotton mixtures, fine wool and dress

English (wadded) quilting

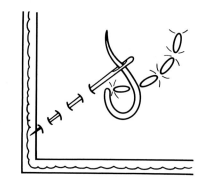

1 Hand stitch through all layers along the marked lines

fabrics are all suitable. These traditional patterns are usually used for decoration and are best worked in a light-weight wadding or domette or even blanket material, which was used in the old days.

For the machine-stitched version, draw your design onto the top fabric and then carefully tack all three layers together. Machine stitch the quilting starting at the centre, using a medium length straight stitch, a zig-zag stitch, a satin stitch or a combination of all three. Machined quilting can take many forms, depending on the use of different techniques, colours and stitching. The top fabric can be silk, cotton, lawn, fine wool, suede, thin leather, dress fabrics or curtain fabrics. The wadding can vary from 57 g (2 oz) to 227 g (8 oz) wadding depending on the depth of padding required.

The backing material for all types of English or wadded quilting can be almost any finely-woven fabric. It is sometimes a good idea to choose a fabric similar to the top layer for a reversible effect in a waistcoat or jacket. As a cover for a cushion, a cheaper fabric such as sheeting or calico is ideal, as it is easy to stitch and unlikely to be seen.

PAINTED QUILTING

Painted quilting is an extension of English or wadded quilting and can also include trapunto, shadow and flat quilting.

Start with a plain fabric such as silk, calico or poplin and paint or print your design onto this. You can use fabric paints or dyes following the manufacturer's instructions for applying and fixing the colours. Artists' acrylic paints are also suitable for things like wall hangings and pictures that do not need frequent washing. You can simply paint your design using a sable watercolour brush, or stamp a design on with a potato cut into a shape and dipped into a dye. There are also silk screen, stencil, batik or tie-dye methods you can choose.

2 Paint the design on to the fabric with a watercolour brush

Painted quilting

When you have created your pattern or picture, treat the fabric according to the manufacturer's instructions for fixing. Press the fabric carefully and follow the basic instructions for English or wadded quilting. You should stitch round your painted shapes to accentuate them and also embellish the whole design with other stitching, embroidery or beadwork. The combinations are myriad and it is worth experimenting to see what you can do.

Small motifs such as flower petals, leaves, butterflies, etc., can be made up separately and stitched onto your work for a three-dimensional effect. Zig-zag stitch round your chosen shape using the English quilting method, and then cut out through all three layers of fabric very close to the stitching. Satin stitch all round to neaten the edge. You can add more painting to include veins in leaves, stamens and any shading together with surface embroidery and beads. Hand stitch these in place on your work, leaving the edges free.

You can make up your own quilted fabric, by machine, using a 57 g (2 oz) or 113 g (4 oz) wadding and a light-weight patterned cotton, silk, or wool top fabric and a plain backing. This is ideal for making table mats, oven-mits, tea-cosies, waistcoats, jackets and children's clothes. You can stitch regular diagonal or vertical and horizontal lines through the layers, preparing the fabrics in the same way as for machined English quilting. Sometimes the pattern of the fabric will help you keep the stitching in regular rows by following a small motif in the design. Otherwise you should draw the initial two intersecting lines and then use a quilting gauge on the machine to keep the lines at a constant distance apart. Always stitch across the centre of the fabric first and then work towards the edges to avoid puckering the

3 Cut away the wadding and backing close to the first row of zig-zag stitching

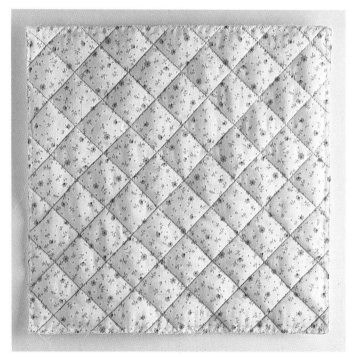

Painting can also be used to great effect when combined with appliqué. This gives a delicate quality to the background and produces softer more natural shapes.

PATTERNED QUILTING
This is yet another version of English or wadded quilting in which patterned fabric is used for the top layer.

Patterned quilting

layers. Use a medium-length straight stitch or zig-zag stitch and keep the lines at least 5 cm (2 in) apart.

You can also use a fabric with an all-over design and just quilt round selected motifs, such as flowers and leaves. Some of these look good with trapunto quilting instead; to really accentuate them, you can then flat quilt the background, again following shapes in the pattern.

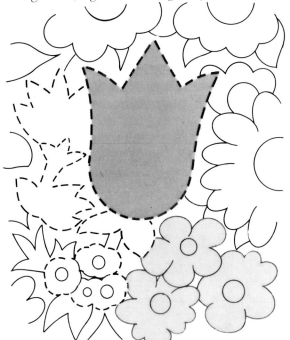

4 Quilt round selected motifs on your patterned fabric

This adds an interesting dimension to the pattern and is suitable for cushion covers, or chair seats.

It is also possible to achieve interesting effects by quilting your own pattern on to a regular striped, spotted or checked fabric. Follow some of the design and then add another dimension with new pattern lines to alter the all-over effect. Pick out squares or add shapes, and experiment with fabrics and designs.

SPRAYED QUILTING

Spray painting can be used in various ways to embellish your quilting. It can be used to accentuate the padding on fabric you have already quilted and also to add patterns and subtle colour changes on your fabric prior to quilting and in conjunction with fabric painting. Use fabric paints and dyes in a spray gun or with a mouth spray diffuser following the manufacturer's instructions for diluting and fixing. Colours can be sprayed on to plain silks and fine cottons in subtle waves of colour for an *ombré* effect and then the fabric can be used for English, Italian or random quilting. You can make simple masks or stencils in paper to cover certain areas of fabric and then spray on your design, moving the mask to repeat a simple shape. When complete, use this fabric for English or trapunto quilting, following and outlining your sprayed designs and embellishing with embroidery and extra stitching lines.

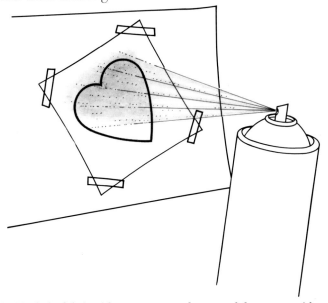

5 Mask the fabric with cut-out paper shapes and then spray with an aerosol or mouth spray diffuser

Sprayed quilting

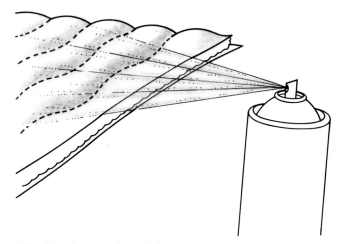

6 *Position the aerosol nearly level with the quilted fabric and spray gently*

Random quilting looks very effective if you spray it after the quilting has been stitched. Hold the spray at a low angle to the fabric thus spraying one side of each little 'hill' of fabric. This has the effect of accentuating the padding and colouring it at the same time. You can also use car spray paints and diluted acrylic paints for pictures, wallhangings, and costumes for fancy dress and the theatre. Experiment with different fabrics and paints for the special effect you want. This sprayed fabric should not be subjected to frequent washing as the dyes are only semi-permanent when used in this way.

RANDOM QUILTING

This is a type of English quilting which is much gentler and less elaborate in its patterns than the type described earlier. It is useful on large areas between very decorative motifs or as an all-over method of quilting for purely functional reasons. It is done in the same way as English quilting, but usually by machine, and it is not always necessary to work out your design beforehand and mark it on to the fabric. It consists of wandering lines weaving over the surface of the fabric at will. Practice will help to keep the stitching even, and avoid getting the lines too close together or too widely spaced. Think of the patterns of ripples in water or the waving lines in the grain of a piece of wood. Start stitching across the centre of the piece of fabric, after thoroughly tacking the top fabric, wadding and backing fabric together. Gradually work outwards, away from your centre line on each side, using a straight machine stitch. Do not stretch or pull the fabric as it goes through the machine or it will pucker. Use a medium to long stitch and light-weight pressure on the presser foot so that you can manoeuvre the fabric easily. Free machine embroidery is also good for this technique as you naturally get a wandering line. It is not so easy to control and really needs to be worked in an embroidery ring or with the backing stiffened with interfacing (or

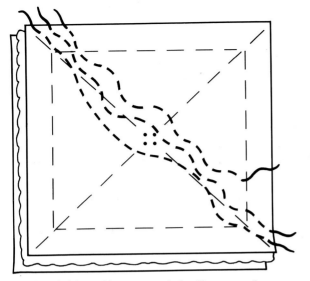

7 Start the stitching with one meandering line across the centre and then stitch more lines towards the edge

even with roller blind spray if it is for a picture or something similar).

You can use most fabrics for this, either plain or sprayed with colours prior to stitching. See the sprayed quilting instructions for details of spraying after stitching for a greater three dimensional effect.

TRAPUNTO QUILTING

Trapunto or stuffed quilting is the high-relief padding of selected areas of your design and it is often combined with other techniques such as painting, flat quilting and quilting patterned fabrics. The top fabric should be a fine closely woven fabric, sometimes stretchy for a high-relief effect. The backing can be a firm, non-fraying fabric or a good quality, open-weave muslin for lighter needs.

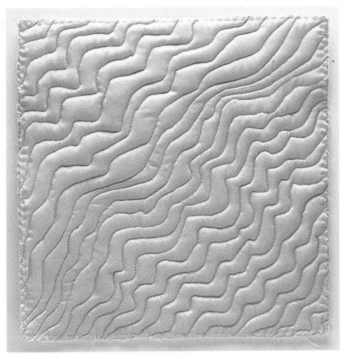

Random quilting

Trapunto quilting

You can mark your design on the top fabric or the backing fabric and then tack the two layers together. Stitch along the design lines using a back stitch or running stitch by hand, or a medium-length machine straight stitch. When you have completed all the stitching, remove the tacking. On the reverse side of the work either part the threads, if you are using a muslin backing, or make a tiny slit in the back of each area to be padded. Gently fill the shape with fluffed out scraps of wadding, pushing it in with a knitting needle or similar, until the shape stands out on the right side. Do not put in too much wadding at a time or it will look lumpy and make sure it is padded evenly right into the corners.

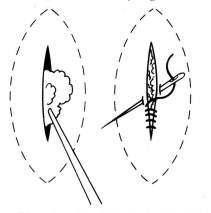

8 Push the wadding through a slit in the backing fabric and then stitch up to neaten

Lastly, pull the muslin threads back into place or stitch up the slit using ladder stitch. By experimenting with different stretchy fabrics and changing the size of the shapes and the amount of padding, you can achieve very subtle or very bold effects, as desired. This technique can be done either on a frame or hand held. When using a frame, the results are generally more satisfactory, as the backing is pulled taut, leaving the top fabric free to show the padded effect.

SHADOW QUILTING

This type of quilting achieves a subtle-coloured design with the use of a transparent top fabric such as chiffon, organdie, net or georgette and brightly-coloured padding with silks and yarns. The backing fabric can be the same for a reversible effect useful on window blinds, screens or lampshades. For other uses, a firm, finely-woven backing is best, as you will use the trapunto and Italian quilting techniques. The top fabric is best in white or very pale pastel colours and the padding and yarns should be very brightly coloured as they will be muted under the top layer.

Follow the trapunto technique using tiny scraps of coloured silk or wadding in the larger areas and the Italian quilting technique in channels using coloured cords and wool.

Shadow quilting

For the reversible shadow quilting, the coloured fabrics, felts and yarns are sandwiched between the two transparent layers and then stitched in position using the flat quilting technique. Tack all the pieces in position on the backing fabric then lay the top fabric over it and tack the layers together all over. Stitch all round each shape by hand or machine adding more stitching lines as desired. If you choose net, you can thread some yarns through afterwards and also embellish the whole design with running stitch in various coloured threads, remembering that the back and front are equally important. Darn in ends of stitching so that they are not visible. This can be combined with painting and spraying techniques for added effect.

9 Tack the fabric shapes to the backing and then place the top fabric over this and stitch round

ITALIAN QUILTING

This is a cross between flat and trapunto quilting with the design stitched on to two layers of fabric in a pattern of parallel lines or channels. These channels are later threaded with wool or cord from the wrong side to give a raised effect.

Transfer your design on to the backing fabric. This can be a good quality muslin or a fairly open weave fabric like linen scrim so that you can part the threads later when inserting the cord. Tack your top fabric to the wrong side of the backing, with right sides outside. Stitch the design from the reverse side, following the pattern. You can use any plain fine fabric, but slightly stretchy ones like crêpe or fine jersey will give a more raised pattern. Straight machine stitch or running stitch by hand are usually employed. Patterns can be very elaborate whether you use traditional designs or modern designs (for example, bold lines for stems, tree trunks, etc.).

When you have completed the stitching remove the tacking threads. Thread a tapestry needle with quilting wool (or something similar like a very thick knitting wool) and insert it through the backing fabric threading it down the channels of the pattern. On curves and at corners, you will have to bring the needle out through the backing fabric and then insert it again into the same hole, leaving a tiny loop of wool at the back. This will allow for any shrinking or pulling of the wool during use and keep the pattern evenly padded.

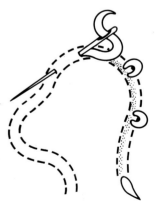

10 Push the needle into the channel, leaving a tail of wool at the end. When you reach a curve, bring out the needle and then insert in into the same hole, leaving a tiny loop of wool.

There is also a method which uses just the top fabric; the quilting wool or cord should be stitched in place by hand. You need to mark out the pattern on the reverse side of the top fabric and then lay the cord or wool between the lines. Hold the cord in place with your left hand and stitch in place with your right hand, using a herring-bone stitch on the wrong side. This stitching should be carefully done to maintain an evenness on the right side, using thread to match the fabric. Where the intersections of the pattern occur, you should cut the cord to avoid any lumpiness. You can also work from the front of the fabric, holding the cord in position with your left hand on the reverse, and stitching it in place from the front. Experiment with both methods, to see which you prefer and make sure that you do not pull the stitches too tight or the fabric will pucker. This type of one-layer quilting should be lined afterwards to protect the stitching.

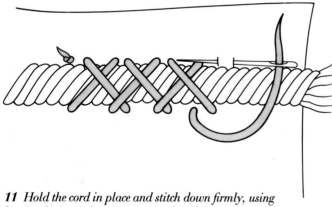

11 *Hold the cord in place and stitch down firmly, using herring-bone stitch on the reverse of the fabric*

Ribbon, stitched in straight lines, can be used successfully using the following technique. Stitch the ribbon on to the right side of the fabric down both sides. Thread your needle with wool or cord and insert it into the channel behind the ribbon. This is particularly attractive

Italian quilting

on a skirt or collar and will have the effect of adding a slight stiffening or body to that part of the garment. It is also a good way of making a frame for a picture or wall hanging, or for finishing different types of quilting.

FLAT QUILTING

This is simply the bonding of two types of fabric with all-over stitching and without wadding between. It is effective for giving extra body to fine fabrics in a decorative way and for bonding a warm fabric to the back of a flimsy one. Mark your design on the top layer, tack the two layers together and then stitch. You can use hand or machine stitch to add embroidery for extra decorative effect.

You can also achieve an exciting, two-colour effect by

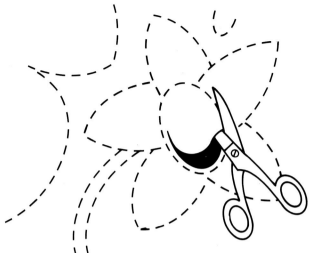

12 Cut away certain areas of the fabric after the stitching is complete

Flat quilting

stitching two layers of different-coloured fabric together and then cutting out selected areas of the top fabric to reveal the backing fabric in little windows. Felt is ideal for the top fabric as it does not fray. If, however, you need to use a washable fabric, you could add blanket stitch round the raw edge to prevent it fraying. The stitching is all important in this technique and you should experiment with different colours, types and thicknesses of thread to achieve a multitude of varied results.

APPLIQUÉ QUILTING

This can be worked in several ways; the idea is to apply shapes of other fabrics on to your top layer of fabric. It adds greatly to the decoration when combined with other quilting methods. You can simply tack your three layers together – top layer, wadding and backing – and then cut out your appliqué shapes in fine fabric and tack them on top, following your design. For a faster method, you can use a light-weight, iron-on bonding fleece to attach the pieces and eliminate the extra tacking. This is a very accurate method as the fabrics cannot move, and it is useful on very fine fabrics as it adds extra body and cuts down fraying. When the pieces are in position, stitch around each appliqué shape with a machine satin stitch, so that the raw edges are completely enclosed. Appliqué pieces should not be smaller than 2.5 cm (1 in) square or they will become too difficult to handle. You can also add a layer of wadding to the back of your appliqué shape, zig-zag stitching it all round the edge before applying it as before. This will give a greater depth of padding when used on larger pieces. Another idea is to pad the appliqué shape and then stitch it to a single layer of top fabric, thus making the quilting in selected areas. This works well using a soft appliqué fabric on a firm, non-stretchy top fabric such as denim, sail cloth or poplin. It is a useful method of adding padded decoration to existing clothing.

13 *Satin stitch round the edge of each appliqué piece to attach, quilt and neaten in one process*

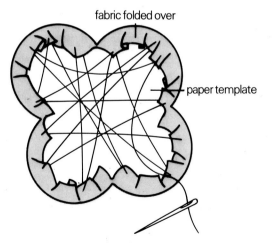

fabric folded over

paper template

14 *An easy way to turn under edges evenly, is to cut out the appliqué shape in card 5 mm (¹/4 in) smaller than the fabric. Draw the edge of the fabric over the card with tacking stitches and then iron in place. Remove the stitching and card and then slip stitch the appliqué piece on the work.*

If you use very fine lawns or silks you can turn under the edge of your appliqué piece and slip stitch it to the top fabric. You can also add padding in this way by pushing in some wadding before the piece is completely stitched all round. If you have machine stitched the tacked pieces in place you can pad these areas using the trapunto method.

Appliqué quilting

TIED QUILTING

This method of quilting for making traditional padded quilts, is particularly used in conjunction with patch-work. But it can also be used for interesting effects in modern designs when mixed with other types of quilting, both on backgrounds and in featured panels. Instead of stitching the layers of fabric and wadding together in lines, individual knots are tied to the backing at regularly spaced points (perhaps the corners of selected patchwork shapes, for example). Traditionally, this was done starting on the wrong side with a long length of thread. Push the needle through to the front, take a small stitch and come out to the back again. Repeat this and then tie the ends in a double knot. Cut off the ends of thread, leaving a little near the knot, to prevent it from coming undone. In modern designs, it is fun to use brightly coloured thread or wool to make tiny spots of colour on a plain ground, quilting the fabrics at the same time. You can also tie the ends at the front of the work to give a different effect. Now, satin ribbon only 1.5 mm ($\frac{1}{16}$ in) wide can be bought, and you can use this threaded on to a tapestry needle for tied quilting. Work the same stitch as described for the thread but starting from the front of the work. After you have knotted the ribbon, tie a tiny bow and trim off the ends neatly. This makes a lovely feature on this type of quilting.

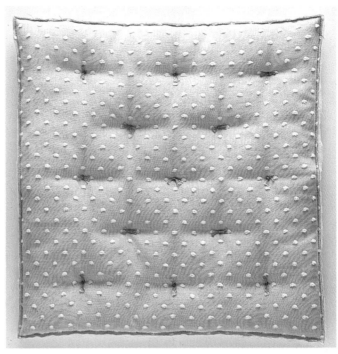

Tied quilting

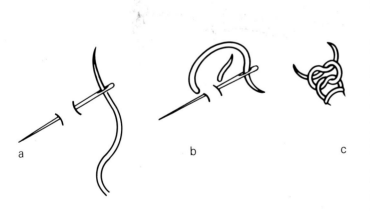

15 a) Push the needle through all the layers to the front of the work, take a stitch and come out at the back again
b) Repeat (a)
c) Tie a double knot and trim off the thread ends

PUFF QUILTING

This is the most thickly padded type of quilting and is ideal for use both in full-size and cot quilts. It is made in squares, using two squares of fabric and some wadding to provide the 'puff'. Work out the finished size for each patch, 10–15 cm (4–6 in) is ideal. Cut out a square template of card or acetate 5 mm ($\frac{1}{4}$ in) larger all round. Use this to mark and cut out the correct number of backing squares. Next make a template for the top fabric squares. This should be about 2 cm ($\frac{3}{4}$ in) larger all round than the backing template. Use this to cut the same number of squares out of your top fabric. Pin the patches together in pairs at the corners, with right sides outside. Make a pleat on the top fabric in the centre of each side of the square, to make it lie flat with the

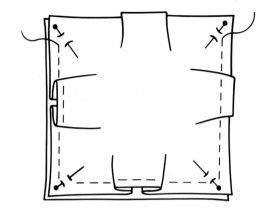

16 *Pin the top square to the backing square at the corners. Make a box pleat, centrally, on all four sides to take in the fullness of the fabric. Tack in place round three sides.*

Puff quilting

backing patch. Stitch round three sides of the square, either by hand or machine, taking 5 mm (¼ in) seams. Insert the wadding through the opening and then stitch up the fourth side. The wadding can be just loose stuffing or a square cut from flat wadding and tucked inside. Make up all the patches in this way ensuring that the amount of padding in each one is the same. Stitch them together in strips, with right sides together, taking 5 mm (¼ in) seams. Press the seams open on the wrong side and then stitch the strips together, matching up the seam lines to form the quilt. This will need to be backed, to hide the raw edges of the seams and the outside edges will have to be bound or turned under. On a large quilt,

join the layers with tied quilting to hold the lining in place. These patches can be made from the same fabric or from different fabrics for a patchwork effect. They should all be of the same weight material like cotton, lawn, dress fabric or silk. The stuffing should be washable, for example, terylene wadding (scraps or cut out squares) or a polyester wadding.

2 TECHNIQUES

PREPARATION

Preparation of the fabrics before you begin any stitching is very important.

Washing

Many cotton and natural fabrics may shrink, or the colour may run, so it is advisable to wash and dry these carefully, prior to making up, to avoid disappointing results when laundering the finished article.

Ironing

Always iron all the fabrics before you start as finished quilting should not be pressed to any degree because it will flatten the wadding. Remember this when you choose your fabrics too, for if the finished article needs frequent washing – as in children's clothing – you should choose a non-creasing fabric such as a polycotton mixture.

Cutting out

The process of quilting tends to reduce the size of your work so you must bear this in mind when cutting out the fabrics. Allow at least 5 cm (2 in) extra, in addition to the seam allowance, all round each piece. When making clothes, pin your pattern to the top fabric and mark all round with tailors chalk so that you can judge where the quilting will fall. Cut out each piece, roughly to shape, leaving the extra fabric all round. Quilt each piece separately and then pin on the pattern again. Cut out and make up the garment following the pattern instructions. You should nearly always cut the backing and wadding larger than the top fabric. Allow enough backing to attach it to the frame if you are using one. You may need to seam pieces together. Do this first with the seams pressed flat and facing the wadding.

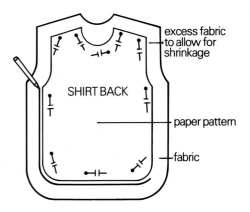

17 Pin the paper pattern on to your fabric. Draw round and cut out, leaving extra fabric to allow for shrinkage when quilted.

MARKING THE DESIGN ON THE FABRIC

There are several methods of marking the quilting designs onto the fabric and I shall describe them in detail here. There are also some things that should not be used.

1. Ball point pens: these are messy, can blob and the ink is very difficult to remove from the fabric.
2. Felt pens: the ink spreads on most fabrics and is difficult to remove.
3. Ordinary carbon paper: this will smudge and the marks on the fabric will not come off easily.
4. Soft pencils: the lines will smudge and make the fabric look dirty.

METHODS

Tracing

This is one of the easiest and quickest methods. It is surprising how transparent fabrics can be, especially plain ones, and it is always worth trying it out. Draw out your design in fine, black waterproof felt pen on white paper. Make sure this is quite dry and place your top fabric over it and tape it in place. If it does not show through well enough, try taping the pattern and then the fabric to a large window. This will make a kind of light box and enable you to trace designs quite successfully. To draw on the pattern, use a hard pencil, embroidery felt pen or watercolour brush and paint. Work on a smooth, hard, flat surface.

Prick & pounce

This is a rather laborious but very successful method that has been employed for several hundred years. Make a tracing of your design (or part of it if it is a repeating one) on good quality tracing paper. Lay the tracing on an old blanket or ironing board and follow the pattern lines, making tiny holes every 3 mm or 4 mm (⅛ in) with a crewel needle. When you have completed this, smooth the back of the tracing paper with very fine sandpaper to remove the tiny pieces of paper pushed through by the needle. Now lay the tracing paper on to your fabric and pin, tape or weight it in position securely. Gently rub talc or chalk (coloured with a little charcoal if necessary) all over the design. (A substance called pounce used to be used but it is difficult to obtain now.) You can distribute the talc with a pad of felt or cotton wool to help force it through the holes. Gently remove the tracing when you have covered the design and, if necessary, join the dots with a fine line of watercolour paint. The advantage of this method is that you are left with a permanent pattern, which can be used over and over again if kept carefully. This is particularly good for designs with a half or quarter repeating motif, as it saves time drawing it out. For an all-over design, you can work directly on to the fabric as follows. Place a thick blanket on your work surface, then your fabric and finally the pattern tracing.

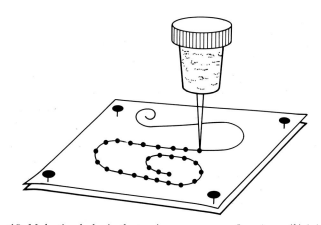

18 *Make tiny holes in the tracing paper, every 3 or 4 mm (⅛ in) using a needle pushed into a cork, for ease of use. Follow the pattern underneath.*

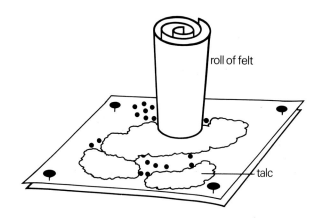

19 *Rub the talc through the holes in the tracing paper using a roll of felt*

Tape, pin or weight the layers securely and then prick the pattern through to the fabric using a very sharp, hard pencil. This will leave a series of tiny pencil dots and also provide you with a permanent pattern in one process.

Trace & tack

A simple design can be drawn on to thin tracing paper or tissue, pinned to your fabric round the edge and then tacked through both layers with small stitches. Take care to finish the ends of tacking securely. Remove the pins, tear away the paper and you are left with your design, in tacking stitches, on the fabric. If you are doing free stitch machine embroidery you can also machine stitch through the paper along the pattern lines and then tear away the paper. This is really only suitable for flat quilting or English quilting when the designs are simple and the padding light.

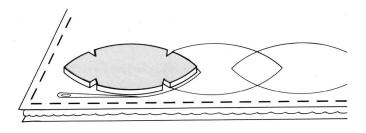

21 Hold the template firmly on to the fabric and run the tapestry needle round it carefully

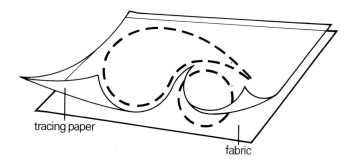

20 Stitch through the tracing paper and fabric along the pattern lines. Pull off the paper carefully when the stitching is complete.

Scratch marking

This method has been used for hundreds of years and is used with templates for the English quilting technique. The three layers (backing, wadding and top fabric) should be tacked together and secured in a frame, if you are using one. Lay the template in position on the top fabric, and run a rug or yarn needle around the template. The needle should be held almost parallel to the surface of the fabric and drawn smoothly round the template.

This leaves a clear indentation which will last a short time, while you hand stitch the quilting. This line will be well pronounced on natural fabrics such as linen, cotton and silk but experiment with man-made fibres, as their tendency to resist creasing may make the line disappear too quickly. Only mark small areas of pattern and stitch them immediately. You can also outline templates with a fine pencil line, a chalk line or using an embroidery felt pen as described. Use the notches in your templates to line up each piece of the pattern correctly and keep the resulting pattern accurate and even.

Masking tape

If you are quilting along straight lines, or perhaps an all-over, criss-cross design, strips of masking tape can be successfully used as a guide. Press the tape on to your top fabric, stitch along one edge and then peel off the tape. Use a quilting gauge or more tape for the other lines of stitching. Do not use masking tape on velvet or velour fabrics as it may pull out areas of the tufted fabric. Always test on spare fabric in case the tape leaves marks when removed.

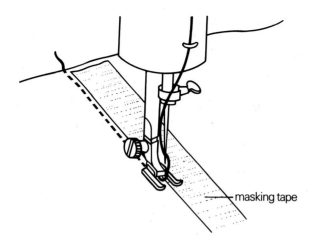

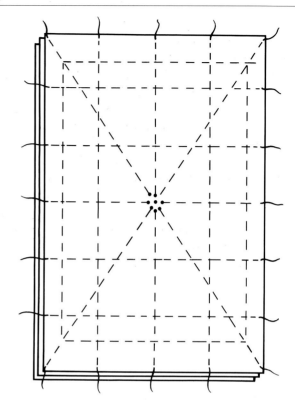

22 Lightly press a strip of masking tape on to the top fabric and use it as a guide along which to stitch

TACKING

This is a very important stage as the layers of backing, wadding and top fabric can easily slip or become pushed out of position while you are stitching. Work on a flat, hard surface or in the frame. Start by pinning the layers together round the edge. Use a very fine needle and thread to avoid leaving marks after the tacking stitches are removed. Start at the centre of the fabric and stitch through all three layers working outward towards each of the four corners. On small pieces of work this will be sufficient to hold it in place but anything larger than about 25 cm (10 in) should have more parallel, horizontal and vertical rows of tacking about every 10 cm (4 in). Use medium length stitches and do not pull the thread too tightly. For flat, Italian and trapunto quilting the amount of tacking can be reduced, as it is the presence of the wadding which causes the fabrics to slip more.

STRETCHING ON A FRAME FOR HAND SEWING

Most pieces of work are quite successful stitched in the

23 Tack from the centre of the fabric out to each corner, then make horizontal and vertical rows of tacking. Lastly, tack all round near the edge.

hand, but stretching your quilting on a frame makes hand stitching easier and it also helps to keep the backing taut. This allows the puffiness of the quilting to be more accentuated on the top surface of the fabric rather than staying evenly distributed. Large pieces of work like quilts are also easier to handle when mounted and rolled on to a frame, leaving a workable area exposed for stitching and the remainder rolled up neatly. Manufactured frames and also a home-made version are described in detail on pages 30–31.

Make sure the width of the frame is large enough to accommodate the width of your work. The length is less important as any length can be wound round the two opposite rollers. Begin with the frame in four pieces. Cut out your backing as described, making sure you follow the grain of the material in both directions. (Pulling a thread, on loosely woven fabrics, is a great help for ensuring a straight line.) Find the centre of one short side of the fabric, mark this, and line it up with the centre of the webbing on one side of the frame. Turn under the edge of the backing and oversew it firmly to the webbing starting from the centre point and working away towards each end. Stitch the opposite side of the fabric to the opposite roller in the same way. Assemble the frame, using the pegs or clamps, rolling any excess backing fabric round the rollers to fit the frame. Do not tension the fabric too much or this will make stitching difficult.

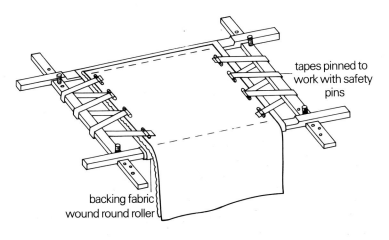

tapes pinned to work with safety pins

backing fabric wound round roller

24 Stitch or staple the backing fabric to the webbing along both short sides. Roll any excess fabric round one roller and then tack the wadding and top fabric in place, leaving the long edge hanging at the front. Pin and tape the sides through all the layers to hold the work taut.

Attach the other two sides of the work using tape, pinning it to the fabrics with safety pins and then wrapping it around the frame. Small pieces of work need not be rolled and the frame can be adjusted to fit exactly by moving the pegs or clamps. Very large frames are either supported by trestles or positioned on the backs of upright chairs, this enables several people to work on one article at the same time.

STITCHING ON QUILTING
The stitching on quilting falls into two main categories, hand stitching and machine stitching. When trying to choose between the two, think first about the results you want to achieve and about the size and type of design on your work. The traditional English quilting was, of course, always done by hand and still should be for a truly authentic look. However, if you have a fairly simple or large scale design, it is quicker and quite satisfactory to work with a sewing machine.

STRETCHING
If you do not use a frame for hand work or you have done machine quilting, you may find that the shape of the work has become distorted after all those rows of stitching in various directions. This can be remedied by stretching as for canvas and embroidery work. You will need a drawing board or wooden work surface, several layers of clean white blotting paper and drawing pins. Place several layers of blotting paper on the wooden work surface to the size of your piece of work. Dampen the blotting paper all over with clean water. Lay the work over the damp blotting paper right side uppermost. Starting at the centre top, pin the work along the top edge along the straight grain of the fabric, stretching it as you go. Repeat this with the opposite side keeping the work pulled taut. Pin the other two sides in the same way pulling the fabric to remove any wrinkles. Leave in a

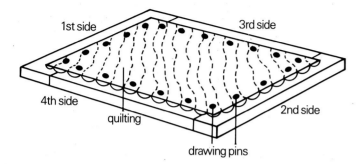

25 *Pin the quilted fabric out over the damp blotting paper on to your board. Start along the top edge and then the opposite side pulling the fabric taut. Work from the centre of each edge. Pin the other two sides in the same way.*

warm atmosphere, not direct heat, until it is quite dry and flat. Remove the pins.

FINISHING
Once you have completed the stitching of your quilted design, there are several ways of finishing off the edges. First cut out the exact size of the finished piece using your paper pattern remembering to add seam allowances. Then follow one of these methods.

Turning in the edges
This is the traditional way of finishing a hand sewn quilt. It is very simple and often the neatest method, particularly on clothing or on an article which has quilting lines parallel to the edge of the work. Pull apart the edges of your work and trim off about 1 cm (⅜ in) of wadding all round. Now fold the top layer of fabric over the wadding about 1 cm (⅜ in), and tuck it inside the backing. Next fold the backing fabric inside, also about 1 cm (⅜ in).

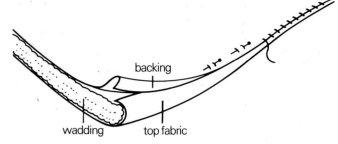

26 *Turning in edges*
Trim off the excess wadding, fold the top layer over the wadding. Turn in the backing and slip stitch to close.

Either pin and slip stitch for an invisible edge, or tack and machine stitch or alternatively, make two rows of running stitches by hand, close to the edge.

Binding the edges
This is useful for clothes and curved edges. Use a ready-made or home-made bias binding which enables you to go round curves smoothly. If you want to bind a quilt or any straight-sided article, a strip of fabric cut on the straight grain is more successful as it will not pull out of shape. Choose the width of binding to complement the size of your work. Also think about the colour; a contrasting plain bias binding is fun for children's clothes and a complementary patterned fabric binding can be very subtle and merge with your design. Home-made binding can be made by cutting bias strips following the method for making piping cord (page 25). Next, fold under the raw edges and press in place. There is a special gadget on the market for doing this. It makes the job much easier and faster (page 32).

After you have made up the article, you will need to trim away the seam allowance on the edges to be bound. Then, with right sides together, open out the binding and stitch it to the raw edge of your work. Stitch along the crease of the binding, then fold it over the raw edge and slip stitch to the backing fabric. You can also machine top stitch the binding in place for a different look. First zig-zag stitch all round the edge of your work to hold the quilting together. Next press the bias binding in half along the length. Slip this over your zig-zag stitched edge and tack carefully in place. Tuck under the raw ends of binding to neaten. Now machine stitch all round, near the edge of the braid, but checking every now and again to ensure you are catching both edges of the braid in the stitching. If you are using straight cut binding, mitre the corners neatly and hand stitch the resulting corner folds neatly on both sides to secure.

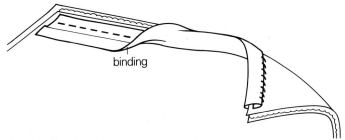

binding

27 *Binding the edge*
Stitch the opened out binding to the front of your work along the fold. Fold the binding over the raw edge and stitch to the backing.

Facing

This is similar to the previous method but the binding is folded right over the edge of the work and hand stitched on to the backing, so that it is completely hidden from the right side. Once again it can be used on quilts, household articles and clothing. Choose bias binding for curved edges and straight grain binding for straight edges. Do not cut off the seam allowance as it will be folded over. Machine stitch the binding to the right side of the work, with right sides facing and raw edges matching. Trim away some wadding and backing fabric

close to the stitching and then fold the binding over to the reverse side of the work. Pin and slip stitch in place. Roll the edge between your finger and thumb, as you go, so that the seam line lies underneath slightly and is hidden from view on the right side.

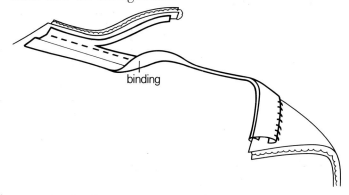

binding

28 *Facing the edge*
Stitch the binding to the front of the fabric along the fold and then trim the seam. Fold the binding over to the back of the work so that the seam line is on the edge of the work. Stitch in place.

Piping

This is generally used for edging cushions and upholstery but can look very attractive in narrower widths on clothing. Piping cord comes in about seven widths and is made of white cotton. You can buy pre-shrunk cord or else wash it yourself before use. You need to cover it with a bias strip of your chosen fabric. To work out the width of the binding, lay your piping cord on to a piece of spare fabric, fold the fabric round the cord and mark 1 cm (½ in) from the cord on both sides of the folded fabric. Open out the fabric and the measurement between the marks is the correct width of bias strip for that particular binding width. To make bias strips, fold your fabric on the cross, matching one straight cut raw edge (the width of your fabric) with one selvedge (the length of your fabric). Press the fold and mark the width of your bias

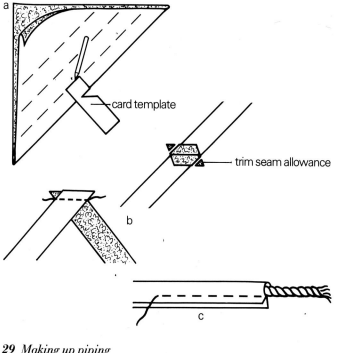

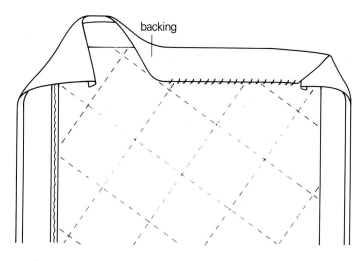

For a garment or quilt edging, stitch the piping just to the top fabric and wadding pulling the backing fabric away so that it does not catch in the stitching. Trim away the wadding close to the stitching, then fold the backing to the inside and slip stitch close to the piping cord to enclose all the raw edges.

Using the backing as a border
This is suitable for straight-sided articles like mats, quilts, hangings and household articles. Trim the wadding so that it extends all round the edge of the work to the chosen width of the border. Trim the backing fabric to twice this width allowing 2 cm (¾ in) for the seam allowance. Press a 1 cm (⅜ in) hem to the wrong side all round and then fold the backing fabric over the wadding and pin to the right side of your work. Slip stitch or machine stitch close to the edge of the backing fabric to

29 *Making up piping*
a) Cut strips of fabric on the cross marking them with a pencil and a card template
b) Join strips, open out, and trim seam edges
c) Fold fabric round cord and stitch in place

strip all along this using a card template as a guide. Cut as many strips as you need and then join them, right sides together. Press the seams open and trim off the surplus points of fabric. Fold this round the cord with the right side outside and machine stitch in place using a zipper foot to keep the stitches near the cord. Stitch this covered cord to the right side of your work matching up the raw edges. For a cushion cover, stitch the piping cord through all the layers of quilting and then stitch the cushion back over the top on three sides. Turn right sides out and insert the cushion pad, then hand stitch to close or alternatively, include a zip in your backing piece.

30 *Backing as a border*
Cut the backing larger than the quilting and fold over a tiny hem all round the backing. Fold over the corners to make mitres and then fold the sides in and stitch to make the border the required width.

enclose the raw edges of fabric. Fold the fabric at the corners into neat mitres and slip stitch in place. You can also use this method for an article that does not have wadding extending beyond the finished size of your work, such as puff quilting. Lay the work on to the wrong side of the backing fabric, cut strips of wadding to the appropriate width and tack them to the edge of your work. Now fold the backing over and stitch as before to make a padded border.

LINING

This is useful if you have used a thin or cheap backing fabric or the trapunto, Italian or tied method of quilting where unsightly stitching shows on the reverse of the work. Cut a piece of lining fabric the same size as your finished quilting, including seam allowances. Lay this on top of the quilting, with right sides facing and pin in place. Stitch all round the edge taking a 1 cm ($\frac{3}{8}$ in) seam and leave an opening large enough to turn the work through to the right side. When you have turned the work right side out, hand stitch the opening to neaten. You can also use this method to attach the backing and wadding to your top fabric prior to quilting. Choose a medium-sized piece of work where the finished size is not crucial, like a wall hanging or mat, as the quilting will make it shrink slightly. Lay the backing fabric and the top fabric together, right sides facing. Lay the wadding on top of the top fabric and tack and stitch through all three layers, leaving an opening for turning. Trim the wadding close to the stitching, turn right sides out and hand stitch the opening to neaten. The quilting can now be done – after tacking all over – through all three layers and there is no need to add anything to finish the edges.

SEAMS

Joining quilting can be done in several ways depending on the finished article and the type of quilting.

For a quilt or large piece of work

The backing pieces should all be joined before tacking the layers together. The top fabrics should also be joined before tacking the layers; this includes any patchwork pieces or the joining of any other top fabric pieces to make up the finished size. For a quilt, have a full width of fabric down the centre of your work and split another width to stitch to each side. This looks better than having a seam right down the middle of your design. Join the pieces with a simple 1 cm ($\frac{3}{8}$ in) seam (right sides together and pressed open flat on the wrong side).

For clothing and smaller articles joined after quilting

There are two methods depending on the article and the type of quilting:

1 *For a backing that will not show* (e.g. clothing needing extra lining etc.)
Join all three layers of each piece, with a 1 cm ($\frac{3}{8}$ in)

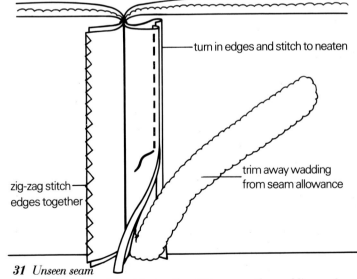

turn in edges and stitch to neaten

trim away wadding from seam allowance

zig-zag stitch edges together

31 *Unseen seam*
Join all the layers right sides together. Trim away the wadding and press seam open. Finish off edges to neaten.

seam, right sides together. Trim away the wadding and press flat. Then pink, zig-zag stitch (or turn under and stitch the raw edges if the fabric frays easily). This can also be slip-stitched to the backing fabric, making sure that the stitches do not come through to the front and that you do not pull them too tightly.

2 For reversible articles
Pull apart the edges of quilting and join only the top fabrics and the wadding. Stitch a 1 cm (3/8 in) seam with right sides together. Open out flat and trim away the surplus wadding as close to the seam as possible. Fold one side of the backing fabric over the seam, then fold over the other side. Turn under the raw edge and slip-stitch in place along the seam line. This makes a very neat hidden seam with all the raw edges enclosed; it is suitable for reversible garments or for articles that you do not want to line.

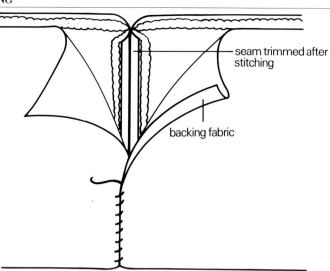

seam trimmed after stitching

backing fabric

32 *Reversible seam*
Pull open the layers of quilting. Stitch the top fabrics and wadding and trim close to the stitching. Fold under the backing fabric and slip stitch to neaten.

3 MATERIALS AND EQUIPMENT

FABRICS
Nowadays, there is an enormous variety of sewing materials on the market, and it is sometimes difficult to decide what to use. There are several hard and fast rules governing the choice of materials for different methods of quilting. I am going to tell you about these and also introduce you to fabrics which can be used in place of traditional ones (Chapter 14). Many of the old fabrics are difficult or even impossible to obtain now and there are plenty of modern alternatives which can turn out even better.

Man-made fibres have helped a great deal with quilting as their crease resistant properties mean that you do not have to worry about ironing the finished product after washing. Washing used to be another problem but with new materials this is seldom difficult, if you follow the directions. Choose the best quality fabric you can afford, after all you will be spending many hours working on it and it would be sad to waste this on a fabric that will not wear well.

Top fabrics
These are for the top layers of your work that will be on show with all the stitching and embroidery. Generally, these need to be slightly stretchy to accommodate the wadding and allow the padded quality of the work to show without puckering. So the more 'give' the fabric has, the more it is suited to trapunto, Italian or thickly padded English quilting.

Backing fabrics

A good backing fabric should always be used to preserve the life of your quilting. It should be of a similar quality as the top fabric, i.e. washable or dry cleanable and can be the same fabric if the work is to be reversible. It should be quite firm so that the quilting is more pronounced on the front of the work. When choosing backing fabric, keep in mind the method you will use to finish the work, as you may want the lining to show as an edging.

Waddings

This is the centre layer of your fabric sandwich, it is used to produce the padded effect of your quilting, as well as for its insulating properties. There are many different types of wadding available nowadays which makes the choice more confusing. Traditionally, wool or cotton was used for wadding, each being available in various forms, but nowadays we generally use the synthetic alternatives. These are much lighter in weight and less dense; they are easy to handle and wash well without going flat or lumpy.

THREADS

As a general rule it is best to match the type of thread, i.e. cotton, synthetic or silk to the type of fabric you are using for your quilting.

Machine quilting

Ordinary dress cottons, cotton-covered polyester and polyester are all suitable and come in a very wide range of colours. You can also get pure silk thread in two thicknesses which, although more expensive, is well worth using for stitching silk fabrics. When using the machine, especially for satin stitch, you should always use the thread to match the fabric or the needle may 'jump' stitches and make untidy gaps in your quilting.

Hand stitching

You can use ordinary dressmaking threads but the stronger quilting thread available is really better. As well as being stronger it is easier to work with, as it is less likely to tangle. It comes in a limited range of colours and is available from specialist shops. For more decorative effects and bolder lines of stitching you can use embroidery threads, stranded cotton (2 or 3 strands), *coton a broder*, silk buttonhole twist and pearl cotton. You can also buy special large spools of light-weight tacking cotton which is cheaper than using ordinary thread and also, being finer, leaves less of a mark on your fabric when removed.

NEEDLES

Hand sewing

All needles should be chosen to go with the thread you are using and also ones that feel comfortable to use. For English quilting, 'betweens', Numbers 7 to 10 are best: sharps for tacking and making up; tapestry needle for threading quilting wool; embroidery crewel needles, for use with thicker threads and decorative stitching; beading needle for stitching on fine beads; a bodkin for threading cord into straight channels; leather needle for leather and suede.

Machine stitching

Choose a machine needle to go with the fabric you are working on: size 9 for very fine fabrics, especially silk; size 11 for light-weight fabrics; size 14 for medium-weight fabrics. For knitted fabrics, a ball-point needle is very helpful as it will not snag the fabric. There is also a special needle for sewing leather and suede, which ensures the holes are punched through successfully. Make sure you use a sharp needle at all times, a blunt one will catch the fabrics and make pulls.

HOOPS AND FRAMES

These are either round or rectangular and the large ones can be supported on specially made stands, or on trestles or chairbacks.

Hoop or tambour frames

These come in various sizes and are suitable for smaller pieces of hand quilting work. You should not use them for heavily padded work or on fabrics that will be marked by the ring. You need a small one for free machine embroidery to keep the fabric taut. The work should be held over the smaller ring and then the larger ring placed over it. The screw is then tightened (not too tightly for hand sewing) to hold the fabric in place.

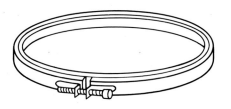

33 Embroidery hoop

Rectangular frames

You can buy several sizes of rectangular frame, some are one permanent size and many have a floor stand for ease of working. They take up a lot of space and are expensive, but they work extremely well. You can make your own version with four pieces of 5 cm × 2.5 cm (2 in × 1 in) timber. Cut all your pieces accurately, to the required size and sand them smooth. Join them securely with flat angle brackets screwed in at each corner. The backing fabric is then stapled on to the frame, all round

the edge. Start at the centre point of one side and work outwards to the corners. Staple the opposite side, stretching the fabric as you go. Staple the other two sides in the same way.

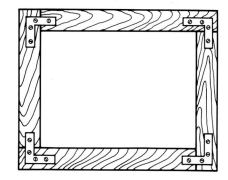

34 Home-made fixed frame with angle brackets holding the corners

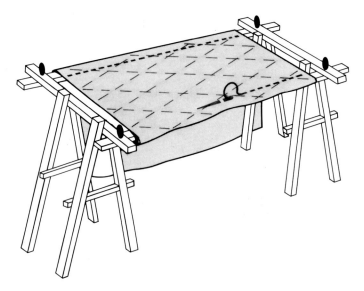

35 Floor standing adjustable frame

Adjustable frames are also available and you can use these for large items such as bed quilts. The frame should be at least the dimension of the width of the quilt. The length of the work is then rolled on to the opposite two sides. These ready-made frames are usually fixed to size with a series of holes in the frame and wooden pegs.

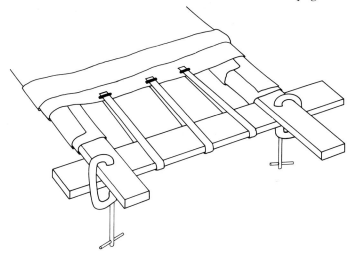

You can make your own version with 5 cm × 2.5 cm (2 in × 1 in) timber sanded and cut to size. Simply overlap the corners and secure them with G clamps. You should wrap the wood with fabric such as ticking or canvas, stapling it in place. The backing fabric is then stitched or stapled to this at the top and bottom. Next, roll the fabric round to a workable size and clamp the frame in position. Wrap white tape round the other pieces of the frame and pin to the sides of the work to stretch it out.

ADDITIONAL EQUIPMENT

Pins
These should be the finest quality dressmakers' pins and sharp enough not to leave marks, particularly on fine fabrics. Glass headed dressmakers' pins are the best, as they are both long and fine, but they are more expensive than ordinary ones. Safety pins are useful for pinning the tapes to the sides of quilting when stretching the work in a frame. Drawing pins are needed to pin out the work when stretching over damp blotting paper.

Tracing paper
This can be bought in various weights in art supply shops and stationers. It comes in pads of different sizes and also in large rolls. This is ideal for tracing your final pattern and the heavy quality tracing paper is best for the prick and pounce patterns which you may want to keep. Roll these up to store them, rather than folding, as tracing paper creases permanently. For preliminary work, greaseproof paper or good quality tissue paper are cheaper alternatives.

Scissors
Ideally, you should have three pairs. One large and sharp for cutting out fabrics, another small with sharp points

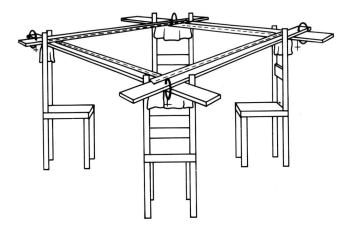

36 Home-made quilting frame, corners held with G clamps

for snipping curves and trimming seams and thread ends, and a third for cutting out paper patterns. Do not be tempted to use the fabric scissors for paper, for the blades are easily blunted making them useless for cutting fine fabrics accurately.

Bias binder maker

A very useful gadget for folding strips of light-weight fabric into accurate width bindings. You cut strips of fabric into bias or straight cut widths and feed them through the gadget. As the fabric comes through the other end, you press it in place with an iron. The gadgets come in two widths to make 2.5 cm (1 in) wide binding and 12 mm (½ in) wide binding. They are available from haberdashery departments and specialist shops.

Templates

You can buy many sorts of templates for quilting and patchwork, as well as making your own from thick card or acetate. Acetate wears better than card so it is preferable for a large job. The advantage of making your own templates is that you can get exactly what you want in terms of size and shape and it is cheaper. There are many sizes and designs ready-made in card, perspex and thin metal and they are worth investing in if you plan to do a lot of work. They are also very accurate.

Transfers

You can buy transfers for patterns to use in quilting in the same way as for embroidery. Iron these on to the fabric to produce a pattern ready for stitching. Take care that the transfer marks do not show through the stitching on the right side; this sometimes happens on light fabrics.

If there is a chance of this only use it for quilting that can be worked from the reverse side such as Italian quilting and some flat and English quilting.

Markers

See Chapter 2 on marking out your design.

Paper-backed fusible fleece

This is very useful for bonding two fabrics together; it should be ironed to the reverse side of the appliqué fabric, the shape should then be cut out and finally the backing paper peeled off. Next, iron the piece in position on to the fabric and leave to cool. The edge may be finished by hand or machine. This method creates a washable joining of the fabrics, thus eliminating tacking. It also cuts down fraying and helps to strengthen fine fabrics.

Light-weight fusible interfacing for patchwork

This interfacing is printed with squares and triangles and seam allowances. You iron the appropriate shapes to the reverse of your fabric and then cut out and stitch the pieces together along the printed lines. It comes in several combinations of shapes, with full instructions. It speeds up the process of patchwork by eliminating the use of templates; it also helps fabric wear well.

In addition, the following equipment may be useful:—
Craft knife
Thimble
Graph paper
Tape
Staple gun

PART II
4 SAMPLER WALL HANGING

The wall hanging is made up of twelve square blocks of stitching each showing a different method of quilting. Each finished block measures approximately 22 cm (8¾ in) square and they are stitched together, in four rows of three squares, to make a panel, about 73 cm × 95 cm (28¾ in × 37½ in) including a border, to finish the edge neatly. The whole panel is suspended from a piece of round wooden dowelling, fed through a channel of fabric, in the top of the hanging. The blocks are all sewn individually and then arranged in a pleasing pattern, to display each to its best advantage. They are then stitched together, backed and a border is added. The channel for the dowelling is made last and stitched to the top of the hanging.

MATERIALS
Twelve 28 cm (11 in) squares of fabric, mostly silks, in various colours to harmonize with each other (for example, pink, green, beige and cream)
Plain poplin and stiff muslin fabric for backing the squares
113 g (4 oz) Terylene wadding 28 cm (11 in) squares and scraps for stuffing
1.5 m (1¾ yd) of plain backing fabric
Thread of all kinds
Acrylic paints and sable brushes
Fabric dyes and sprays
Yarns and quilting wool
Scraps of coloured silk and net
Various markers
Stiff card for templates and a sharp craft knife
A piece of 2.5 cm (1 in) dowelling and about 83 cm (32½ in) long (a broom handle cut to length is ideal)

MAKING UP THE INDIVIDUAL BLOCKS

Random quilting block
Tack together a 29 cm (11 in) square of silk, with a square of poplin with a square of 113 g (4 oz) wadding in between. Right sides of the fabrics should be outside. Mark a wandering line diagonally across the fabric from corner to corner using an embroidery felt pen. With a straight, fairly long machine stitch, sew along this line first. Choose the thread colour to tone or contrast as desired. Now sew other lines on either side of the central line, similar to the lines in the grain of wood. There is no need to mark these on the fabric first, unless you want to. Sometimes the freedom of blank fabric produces a more natural design and a flowing line. Stitch right to the edge of the fabric with each line, leave the needle in the fabric and then turn the work round and begin the next line. This cuts down on thread ends. Remove the tacking and stretch the quilting, if necessary, to flatten it, using damp blotting paper (page 23). Next cut out an accurate 24 cm (9½ in) square from the fabric. Zig-zag stitch all round the edge to neaten.

Puff quilting block
Using a craft knife and a set square, accurately cut out two card templates. Cut one 9 cm (3½ in) square and the other 11 cm (4¼ in) square. Use the smaller square to draw round and cut out nine squares of poplin backing fabric. Use the larger square to draw round and cut out three squares of pink, three squares of peach, and three squares of rose-pink Habotai silk. Take one silk square and pin it to one backing square at the corners, right sides outside. Match up the corners carefully and

make a box pleat in each side, to take in the fullness of the silk square. Stitch round three sides, 5 mm (¼ in) from the raw edge, and then fill with wadding. Stitch up the fourth side of the square. Repeat this with the other eight squares of silk. Arrange the squares into three rows, so that no two squares of the same colour are next to each other. Stitch the three squares together in each row and then stitch the three rows together. Keep the seams at an accurate 5 mm (¼ in) so that all the seams line up. Press open the seams and then zig-zag stitch all round the edge of the whole square to neaten.

Shadow quilting block
Draw out the design to full size using black waterproof felt pen on white cartridge paper. Follow the square by square method to enlarge the design. Cut out a square of white organza and one of white poplin, both measuring 28 cm (11 in). Trace the design on to the organza, very lightly, with a sharp pencil. Trace off the leaf shapes on to tracing paper and cut them out in various green fabrics. Tack these in position on to the underside of the organza. Now place the poplin on the back of the organza and tack the layers together all round the edge

37 Design for shadow quilting, each square represents 2 cm (¾ in)

and across the centre. Stitch all round the outlines of the design, in appropriate-coloured thread, either by hand or on the sewing machine and then remove the tacking. Add veins to the leaves with stem stitch. Snip a tiny hole in the poplin, behind the flower shapes and stuff these areas with different, brightly-coloured scraps of Habotai silk, to give colour to the petals. When you have done this, stitch up the slits in the poplin with oversewing or ladder stitch. Carefully cut out the quilting to an accurate 24 cm (9½ in) square and zig-zag stitch all round the edge.

Sprayed quilting block

Enlarge the heart shape and transfer it to the centre of a piece of cartridge paper, about 30 cm (12 in) square. Using a craft knife, cut out the shape carefully. Take one of the 28 cm (11 in) squares of pale silk, iron it and fix it to your work surface with masking tape or pins. Using the heart shape, lay the mask over the fabric and spray lightly with spray paint. As this is a wall hanging you can use car spray paints or mix up fabric paints to a thin consistency and use a diffuser or aerosol spray. Just hold the mask in position with your fingertips. Spray on the paint in a fine layer. When the first spraying has dried, spray a different colour over the top. Remove the mask and lay the paper heart shape directly over the heart on the fabric and spray with another colour round the edge to complete the design. Leave to dry thoroughly. Now, with right sides outside, place this square of sprayed silk over a poplin backing square, with a square of 113 g (4 oz) terylene wadding sandwiched between them. Tack them together, across the centre and round the edge. Stitch round your sprayed design to quilt it following the outer edges of the heart shape with several rows of stitching. Choose soft, complementary-coloured threads, to blend in with the design, stitching by hand or machine. Add some extra stitching to decorate inside the

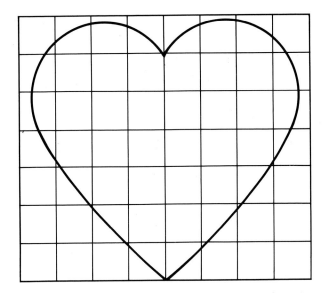

38 *Template for sprayed quilting, each square represents 2 cm (¾ in)*

sprayed shape. Remove the tacking and cut the quilting to an accurate 24 cm (8½ in) square. Zig-zag stitch all round the raw edge, to neaten.

Patterned quilting block

Cut out a 28 cm (11 in) square of light-weight fabric patterned with a small, regular design. Lay this on top of a similar-sized square of poplin backing fabric with 113 g (4 oz) wadding sandwiched between. Make sure the right sides are outside. Tack the layers together, across the centre and round the edge. Using a strip of masking tape, or following the design, machine stitch a straight line diagonally across from one corner to the other. Stitch another diagonal line to cross this. Gradually stitch all over the fabric in straight, diagonal lines working from the centre lines outwards. Use the design of the fabric to guide you or else use a quilting gauge to keep the lines parallel. Do not make the lines of stitching too close together, or you will flatten the quilting too much and distort it. Remove the tacking stitches, cut the quilted square to an accurate 24 cm (9½ in) and zig-zag stitch all round to neaten.

Trapunto quilting block

Using a black waterproof felt pen, draw out the design (page 67) to full size on cartridge paper following the squaring up method. Take a 28 cm (11 in) square of the backing fabric and trace the design through with a sharp pencil. Lay the square of crêpe de chine on the back of this, matching up the raw edges with right sides outside. Tack the two layers together, across the centre and round the edge. Working from the wrong side of the work – with the backing fabric uppermost – stitch all round, following the design outlines, in a slightly darker-coloured thread. When you have completed this, remove all the tacking threads. Using very sharp, pointed embroidery scissors, snip a tiny hole in the backing fabric only, in each of the large areas of the design. Tease out scrap pieces of terylene wadding and push these into the back of the design, to pad it. Use a bodkin or knitting-needle and make sure you are padding evenly and not excessively. When all the necessary areas are padded, stitch up the slits by hand, using oversewing or ladder stitch. Cut the quilting to an accurate 24 cm (9½ in) square and then zig-zag stitch all round the edge to neaten.

Tied quilting block

Cut out a square measuring 28 cm (11 in) of spotted white cotton voile. Cut out similar-sized squares of pink Habotai silk 113 g (4 oz), terylene wadding and poplin backing. After pressing, lay them flat on the work surface in this order – poplin, wadding, silk and voile (right sides outside). Tack them together, across the centre and around the edge. Using the spots in the fabric as a guide, mark points at regular intervals for tie quilting. Thread your needle with stranded embroidery silk in one of several colours. Working from the right side of the fabric – with the voile on top – push the needle through all the layers to the back, leaving a length of silk at the front. Take a tiny stitch and then tie the ends of the silk in a double knot. Trim off the ends about 5 mm (¼ in) from the knot to leave a tiny coloured tassel. Repeat this all over the square at the other marks, with different coloured embroidery silks. This will leave you with tiny coloured tassels quilting your fabric. Remove the tacking and cut the square to an accurate 24 cm (9½ in) square. Zig-zag stitch the raw edges to neaten.

English quilting block

Use a small frame for this project. Mount a square of backing fabric into the frame (page 30). Lay a 28 cm (11 in) square of 113 g (4 oz) terylene wadding centrally on top of this and then a similar-sized square of silk. Tack them together diagonally across the centre and around the edge. Trace off the heart-shaped template (page 68) and use this tracing to cut your own templates from stiff card or acetate. Lay the template in position and mark it with the scratch method (page 21) using a yarn needle. Stitch around this shape by hand in tiny running stitches, using a matching thread. Fill in the central stitching then mark and stitch, using a ruler for the diagonal lines, until you have built up the whole design with a 24 cm (9½ in) square area. Remove the work from the frame and take out the tacking stitches. Cut out an exact 24 cm (9½ in) square of the quilting and zig-zag stitch all round the raw edges to neaten.

Italian quilting block

Trace off the design from page 69. Cut out a 28 cm (11 in) square of stiff muslin backing fabric and using dressmakers' carbon paper and a sharp pencil go over the design tracing, to transfer the design on to the fabric.

Repeat this three more times, replacing the tracing in the correct position each time and fixing with pins or tape. Place the 28 cm (11 in) square of silk on the back of this, with right sides outside, and tack them together across the centre and round the edge. You can use a frame for this if you like, see page 30 for details of mounting in a frame. Using a matching thread and a tiny running stitch, hand stitch all round the design from the reverse of the fabric. Keep turning the work over to make sure you are keeping the stitching even. Remove all the tacking when the stitching is complete. Thread a yarn needle with quilting wool and pad the channels of the design with this. When you reach a curve, bring the needle out through the backing fabric and replace it into the same hole, pushing the needle forward a little way and out again, to negotiate the curve. Leave a tiny loop of wool at the back of the work to allow for shrinkage and evenness of padding. When you have finished the padding, cut out the quilting to an accurate 24 cm (9½ in) square. Zig-zag stitch all round the edge to neaten.

Flat quilting

Cut out two 28 cm (11 in) squares of felt, one in pink and one in beige. Draw out the design (page 70) to the correct size on to thin tracing paper using the enlarging squares method. Place the two squares of felt together, beige on top, and then put the pattern on top of these. Tack all three layers together, across the centre and around the edge. Now, using a straight stitch, machine carefully round all the pattern lines through the tracing paper. When you have finished stitching, remove all the tacking and tie off the threads at the back of the work. Carefully tear away the tracing paper to leave the stitching on the felt. Using the pattern as a guide, carefully cut out the shaded areas on the top fabric only, leaving the backing felt colour showing through. Use very sharp, pointed embroidery scissors and try to cut as close to the line of stitches as possible. Cut your felt to a 24 cm (9½ in) square and zig-zag stitch round the edge to neaten.

Painted quilting block

Draw out the design (page 71) to full size on to the centre of a large sheet of clean, white blotting paper, using the square enlarging method and a very fine black waterproof felt pen. Lay the 28 cm (11 in) square of white silk over this and fix it in place on to the work surface with drawing pins. Mix up your acrylic paints with water, to a fairly liquid consistency and start by painting the central motif on to the silk. Follow the design which is through the fabric. Use a medium-sized, sable water-colour brush and work quite quickly. Leave this a few minutes to dry and then paint the next colour round it. Leave this to dry and continue painting the colours, following round the central shape in bands of varying widths. Try letting some of the colours flow into each other by painting the next band before the first colour has dried completely. This will give you a less defined, watery look which is very pretty. Leave the painted fabric to dry completely, pinned to the work surface. Now place the painted square of silk over a similar-sized square of 113 g (4 oz) terylene wadding and below this place a square of poplin backing fabric. Tack the three layers together across the centre and around the edge. Now stitch around the edge of the central motif, using a straight stitch on the machine. Stitch the centre of the flower in the same way. Change to a medium-width, zig-zag stitch and sew round the bands of colour to quilt the fabrics. Add hand stitching – stem stitch and satin stitch – to represent stamens in the centre of the flower. Remove the tacking stitches and cut out the quilting to an accurate 24 cm (9½ in). Zig-zag stitch the raw edges to neaten.

Appliqué quilting block

Draw out the design (page 72) to full size on to tracing paper using the squaring up method. Turn the tracing over to the reverse side and trace off each separate element of the design on to the backing paper of separate pieces of fusible fleece. Number them, for identification purposes later, both on the fusible fleece and on the design tracing. Choose a fabric for each piece and cut it out, roughly to size. The fabrics should be fine silk or lawn so that the work does not become too thick. Iron the corresponding Bondaweb shape to the wrong side of your appliqué fabric following the manufacturer's instructions. Leave to cool and then cut out the shape following your drawn pencil line. Peel off the backing paper and lay down the appliqué piece on to your 28 cm (11 in) square of fabric, in the correct place. Iron to bond. Repeat this with all the other appliqué shapes and build up your design until it is complete. Lay this square of appliquéd fabric over a similar-sized piece of 113 g (4 oz) terylene wadding and then lay these two layers on to a square of poplin backing fabric. Tack the layers together, across the centre and round the edge. Now stitch round each appliqué shape using appropriate coloured thread and a machine satin stitch. Make sure the stitching completely covers the raw edges of the fabric shapes. Cut the quilting to an accurate 24 cm (9½ in) square and zig-zag stitch round the edge to neaten.

TO MAKE UP THE WALL HANGING

The wall hanging is made up of these twelve quilted blocks stitched together in four horizontal rows of three blocks each. Lay all your blocks out on the work surface and put them into a pleasing arrangement. Try to keep the colours evenly distributed and take the various design elements into account as you arrange them. When you have decided where each block is to be placed, pin the three blocks in the bottom row together. Stitch these, right sides together and taking 1 cm (⅜ in) seams. Use a straight machine stitch or hand running stitch. Stitch the

three blocks in the other three rows together in the same way and then press open the seams on the reverse. Now pin and stitch the rows together, taking 1 cm (⅜ in) seams and lining up the edges of the squares. Press the seams open on the reverse.

Press the backing fabric and lay it out on your work surface, wrong side up. Lay the wall hanging centrally on top, right side up and pin in place. Trim the backing fabric so that it is 8 cm (3½ in) larger all round than the padded piece. Cut four 3.5 cm (1½ in) wide strips of 113 g (4 oz) terylene wadding to fit around the outside edge of the padded piece. Trim the wadding at the

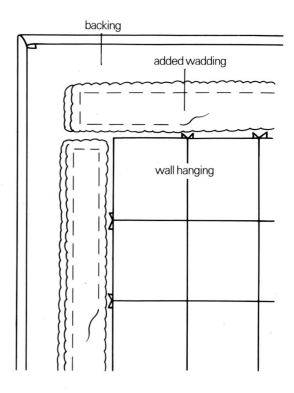

39 *Adding the wadding strips to pad the border of the wall hanging*

corners to fit accurately. Tack these in place round the outer edge of the quilted piece. Now fold the backing fabric over the wadding, turn under a small hem and tack the fabric in place on the front of the wall hanging. Make sure all the raw edges of wadding and fabric are covered. At the corners, fold the fabric under neatly, to form mitres. Trim away any excess fabric from the corners and hand stitch the mitres neatly.

Now machine stitch along all the seam lines to join the padded part to the backing fabric. Start at the centre and work outwards. Hand stitch the edge of the border in place all round. Cut a strip of the backing fabric 68 cm × 16 cm (26¾ in × 6½ in). Turn a 1 cm (⅜ in) hem under on the two short ends and machine stitch in place. Fold the fabric along the length, right sides outside, so that the raw edges are level. Stitch this centrally to the back of the hanging along the line where

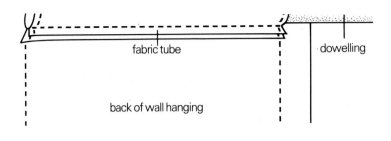

40 *Stitch the tube of fabric to the top of the wall hanging, on the reverse side*

the border meets the padded area on the top edge. Insert the dowel into this channel and suspend the wall hanging on two large hooks screwed into the wall.

5 QUILTED SCALLOP-EDGED EVENING JACKET

This is a quilted, bolero-style jacket with sleeves ending just below the elbow. Made in peach-coloured silk taffeta, it is an ideal jacket to go over a strappy cocktail dress. You could also make it more exotic for evening wear by choosing a dramatic-coloured fabric and adding bugle beads stitched along the quilting lines. A contrasting lining fabric would also be pretty. Conversely, if you made it in a fine cotton print, it would be a useful jacket to go over a pretty sundress. The scallop-edge is stitched first and then the fabrics are turned right sides out. The pieces are then quilted through the lining, wadding and top fabric. The jacket pieces are then cut out accurately and stitched together. The seams are finished inside, by hand, to enclose all the raw edges. The pattern is given on a squared grid in one size to fit 12–14.

MATERIALS

1.50 m (1½ yd) of peach-coloured, light-weight silk taffeta 90 cm (36 in) width
1.50 m (1½ yd) of matching Habotai silk 90 cm (36 in) width
1.50 m (1½ yd) of 57 g (2 oz) terylene wadding
Dressmakers' graph paper and sharp 2H pencil
White cartridge paper to make pattern
Matching silk thread
Pattern (see pages 74–75)

MAKING UP

(1.5 cm (⅝ in) seam allowance throughout)
Using our squared diagram, draw out the jacket pattern to full size on to dressmakers' graph paper. Each square

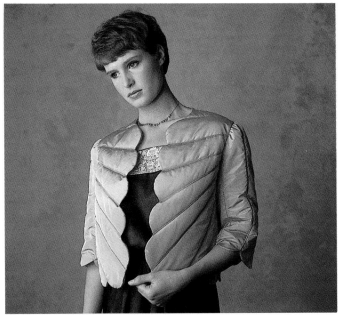

Quilted scallop-edged evening jacket

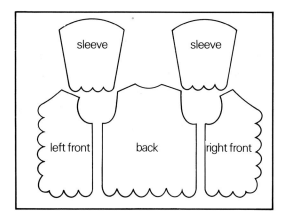

41 *Layout for pattern pieces*

equals 5 cm (2 in). Draw round a cup or similar circular object to help get the scallop-edge accurate and to form smooth curves. Mark the quilting lines on to the pattern pieces and then cut the pieces out round the outlines. Lay the pieces on to the reverse side of your taffeta, as shown in the layout diagram. Using a very sharp pencil, draw on to the fabric along the dotted lines around the neck and along the scallop-edges on all the pieces. This is your stitching line. Then make a pencil mark for the ends of the quilting lines. These will be joined to the points of the scallops with a ruled line on the right side of the fabric later.

Now cut out the fabric about 2.5 cm (1 in) outside the edge of the pattern. Remove the pattern pieces, turn over the sleeve and front pieces, and pin on and cut out one more front and one more sleeve from the remaining fabric. Pin the pattern on to the reverse side of the fabric,

as before. Draw round the neck edge and scallops and cut out as before. Now remove the pattern pieces and use them in the same way to cut out all the pieces from the wadding and from the lining fabric. Do not mark these fabrics, just cut them out roughly to shape about 2.5 cm (1 in) outside the patterns.

Take one sleeve piece, in each of the three materials. Lay the wadding piece down first, then the lining (right side uppermost) and then the top fabric (wrong side uppermost). Carefully tack these pieces together round the edge, using a very fine needle and cotton, as the taffeta marks easily. Now machine stitch all along your pencilled line round the scallops. Use matching thread and small straight stitches. Trim the seam allowance very close to the stitching and snip right into the points of the scallops with the points of your needlework scissors. Remove the tacking stitches. Turn the sleeve right sides out so that the wadding is between the lining and the top fabric. Roll the seam edge of the scallops, between your finger and thumb, to bring the seam right on to the edge of the sleeve and then press lightly in place. Tack the three layers of fabric together all round the edge and across the centre to stop them from slipping.

Using a ruler and a very sharp pencil, gently draw in the quilting lines, from the points of the scallops to the marks taken from the edge of the pattern. Stitch along these lines using matching or contrasting silk thread. You can use a straight machine stitch or a narrow, machine satin stitch. Start by stitching the middle rows and then the outer ones, beginning each row at the point of the scallop. Pull the threads to the back of the work and tie off neatly. Treat all the other jacket pieces in the same way, stitching around the neck edge as well, on the fronts and back. Turn the fabrics, press, tack and stitch the quilting lines as before.

When you have completed the quilting, tie off all the threads at the back. Lay the paper pattern pieces back on to the quilted fabric and pin round the edge carefully matching up the scallops. Cut out the raw edges of the jacket accurately and mark in the notches from the pattern. Unpin the pattern.

Now match up the shoulder seams and pin and stitch the two fronts to the back, with right sides together, and taking 1.5 cm (⅝ in) seams. Make sure the finished neck edges match up exactly. Trim away the layers of fabric at the seams quite close to the stitching, leaving one lining fabric seam allowance the full width. Turn the raw edge of this under and pin and slip stitch it over the raw seam edges to enclose them neatly. Press lightly on the wrong side.

On the side seams of both the fronts, you will have marked two notches. Sew two rows of running stitches between these notches and pull up the threads slightly, to make the side seams fit the jacket back. This gives a slight shaping for the bust on the front of the jacket without putting in darts, which would spoil your quilting. With right sides together, pin the front and back side seams matching the scallops accurately. Stitch in place and then trim and neaten as for the shoulder seams.

Take one sleeve and with right sides together, pin the

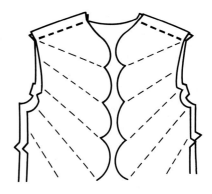

42 Stitch the fronts to the back at shoulder seam, with right sides facing

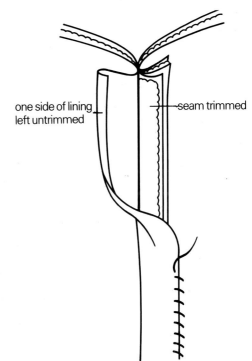

43 Finish the seams by trimming all layers except for one lining layer. Turn the raw edge under and then fold it over the raw seam edges to cover them.

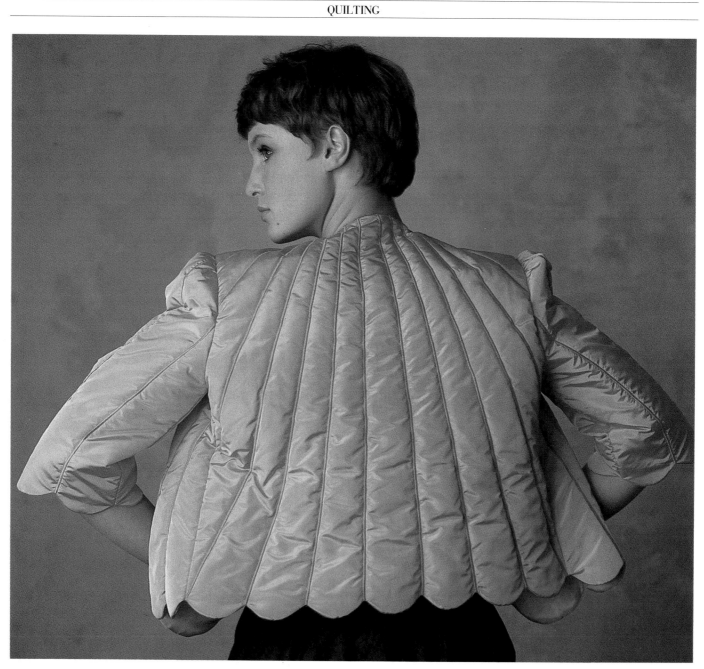

Quilted scallop-edged evening jacket (back)

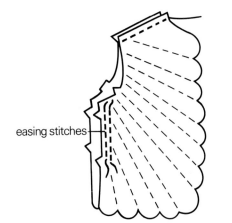

44 *Pull up the easing stitches to make the front fit the back of the jacket at the side seams*

underarm seam matching up the scallops at the cuff edge. Stitch and then trim and finish the seam as before. Run two rows of gathering stitches between the notches

on the head of the sleeve. Pull up the gathers slightly, until the notches match up with the ones on the armhole edge. Slip the sleeve in to the armhole, with right sides together. Pin and tack in place. Stitch the sleeve in place taking a 1.5 cm (⅝ in) seam. Finish the seam as before on the inside of the jacket. Repeat with the other sleeve to complete the jacket. Turn right sides out and then gently press the seams, only, on the outside of the jacket.

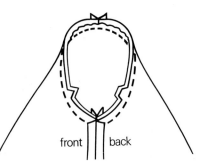

45 *Slip the sleeve into the armhole, match up the notches, and tack in place*

front | back

6 ITALIAN QUILTED CUSHION COVER

This cushion cover is made in grey wild silk with satin ribbon, in various shades of grey and white, stitched on top. It is sewn diagonally, in channels of varying widths and then these channels are threaded with quilting wool, for padding. The backing is a stiff muslin and the stitching is done by machine. The edge of the cushion is piped with cord covered in the same grey silk. This is a modern way of using the old Italian quilting technique. The cushion is 46 cm (18 in) square.

MATERIALS
1 m (1¼ yd) grey wild silk

50 cm (20 in) square of stiff muslin or poplin backing fabric
2 m (2¼ yd) medium-width piping cord
Quilting wool and a yarn needle or bodkin
Satin ribbon, in varying widths and colours of grey and white
46 cm (18 in) square, feather-filled, cushion pad
Matching threads

MAKING UP
(1 cm (⅜ in) seam allowance throughout)
Cut out a 50 cm (20 in) square of the grey silk. Iron it

A selection of quilted cushion covers: clockwise, from top left – *Italian quilted, painted, patterned, and random quilted and sprayed.*

and then lay it out on your work surface. Take a selection of the satin ribbons and lay pieces out, diagonally, across the fabric until you have a satisfactory arrangement. Do not use too many strips of ribbon, or you will hide too much of the fabric. Tack the ribbons in position and trim off the ends, level with the fabric square. Cut out a 50 cm (20 in) square of the muslin backing fabric and lay this under the silk. Match up the raw edges and tack this in position across the centre and round the edge. Now machine stitch down both sides of the ribbons, as close to the edge as you can. Next, using a quilting gauge on your sewing machine, stitch channels of varying widths between the ribbons. The quilting gauge will help you to keep the stitching lines parallel to each other. Do not make any of the channels narrower than 5 mm (¼ in) or wider than 2.5 cm (1 in). Start the stitching across the centre of the cushion and work out, towards the corners. Remove the tacking. Now thread a yarn needle or long bodkin with quilting wool and thread this through the channels. Some of the wider channels will need several strands of wool to pad them. Thread wool through the channels behind all the ribbons, except the very narrow ones. Push the bodkin between the ribbon and the silk, or this padding will show at the back of the work more

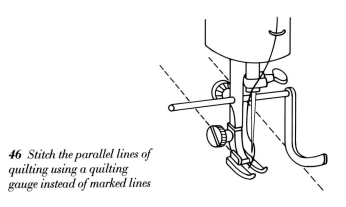

46 Stitch the parallel lines of quilting using a quilting gauge instead of marked lines

than at the front. Some channels may look good unpadded so try this out. When you have completed the padding, cut the square of fabric to an accurate 46 cm (18 in) square and zig-zag stitch all round the edge.

Cut bias strips of the remaining silk fabric, join them and use this to cover the piping cord (page 25). With raw edges matching, machine stitch the covered piping cord around the padded cushion cover front, on the right side. Cut a 46 cm (18 in) square of the grey silk for the back of the cushion cover and make up the cover as for the patterned cushion cover.

7 PATTERNED CUSHION

This cushion cover features the patterned quilting technique. I have chosen a grey, floral, light-weight dress fabric and a medium-weight wadding for this. The quilted part forms the front of the cushion while the back of the cover is made from the plain fabric. The cover is finished with a piped edge, in plain grey silk, which attractively completes the effect. The instructions are for a 46 cm (18 in) square cushion pad.

MATERIALS
50 cm (¾ yd) of grey, patterned dress fabric
A 50 cm (20 in) square of poplin backing fabric
A 50 cm (20 in) square of 113 g (4 oz) terylene wadding
2 m (2¼ yd) of piping cord (medium thickness)
Plain grey silk to cover piping cord
One 46 cm (18 in) square feather cushion pad
Matching grey thread

MAKING UP

Iron all your fabrics. Lay the backing fabric, wrong side uppermost, on to your work surface. Next, put on the wadding and then a 50 cm (20 in) square of the patterned fabric, right side uppermost. Tack all the layers together carefully as described in the preparation of fabrics (page 22). Using a medium length, straight machine stitch, machine round all the motifs, starting at the centre of the fabric and working outwards. Sew round each flower and leaf using a matching grey thread to quilt the fabric. The areas where the stitching is close together, like the leaves, will become flatter but by just sewing round the outlines of the flowers you will be able to make them stand out more from the surface. You can further accentuate the flowers by adding surface embroidery, if you like, and perhaps tiny beads as well.

Remove all the tacking stitches when the quilting is complete and cut the fabric to a 46 cm (18 in) square. Cover the piping cord with bias strips of plain, grey silk and stitch in place following the details on finishing (page 25). Pin and tack the piping cord round the edge of your quilted square on the right side, matching up the raw edges. Where the ends of the cord meet, push back the covering, snip the ends of the cord to fit together exactly and then pull the ends of covering back. Overlap these to make a neat finish. Cut another 46 cm (18 in) square of the patterned fabric and place this, right sides together over your quilted piece. Tack in place all round and then stitch with a straight machine stitch through all the layers taking a 1 cm (½ in) seam. Stitch round three sides and just round the corners to leave a gap for inserting the cushion pad. Trim the surplus fabric from the seams at the corners and turn the cover right sides out. Insert the cushion pad and turn in the raw edges of the fabric at the opening. Hand stitch this opening to neaten, making tiny slip stitches close to the back of the piping. You can also insert a zip into the centre of the backing fabric before

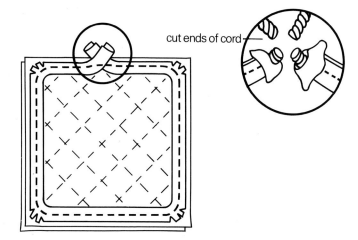

cut ends of cord

47 *Stitch the covered piping cord all round the edge of the cushion cover. Overlap the ends of the piping after trimming the cord inside (close-up).*

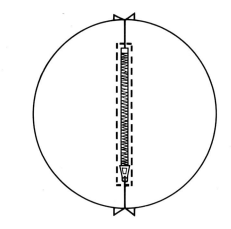

48 *Insert a zip into the centre of the back of your cushion cover before cutting out the correct shape and stitching to the cover front*

stitching the cover together. If you do this you can sew round all four sides and then open the zip to insert the cushion pad. This is also useful for washing the cover later.

8 RANDOM QUILTED AND SPRAYED CUSHION COVER

This round cushion cover is made from plain silk which has been sprayed with fabric dyes, prior to stitching. The layers are then assembled and the cover is quilted with random lines of stitching.

MATERIALS

60 cm (¾ yd) Macclesfield silk in white, cream or a very pale colour
A 40 cm (16 in) square of calico or poplin backing fabric
A 40 cm (16 in) square of 113 g (4 oz) terylene wadding
Fabric dyes, paints or inks
1 round cushion pad 38 cm (15 in) diameter
A mouth spray diffuser or spray gun, with aerosol canister and some spare paint jars – both available from large art shops
Clean white blotting paper
Various threads
Drawing pins, a pair of compasses and cartridge paper

MAKING UP

(1 cm (⅜ in) seam allowance throughout)
Cut out a 40 cm (16 in) square of the silk, to make the front of the cushion cover. Stretch the ironed square of silk over a square of blotting paper 60 cm (25 in) and secure in place with drawing pins. Using a spray kit (or mouth spray diffuser for a speckled effect) apply blending colours in the design of your choice. Now pile the 40 cm (16 in) squares in this order: backing (wrong side up); wadding; sprayed silk (right side up).

Match up the raw edges and tack the layers together across the centre and round the edge. Now machine stitch the quilting. Start with a central, diagonal, gently waving line and gradually work towards the edges with flowing lines to follow and complement each other. You can use a mixture of straight, zig-zag and satin stitches in

varying shades of thread, depending on the finished effect that you want.

When you have finished the stitching, remove the tacking and pin the quilting taut over clean, damp blotting paper to stretch it back to shape (see page 23). While it is pinned out like this, you can prepare a slightly darker coloured dye or ink and fill your spray gun with this. Put the nozzle of the spray gun nearly down to the level of the quilting and spray gently, from side to side, to colour the near side of each little mound made by the quilting. Do not spray too much, or you will spoil the

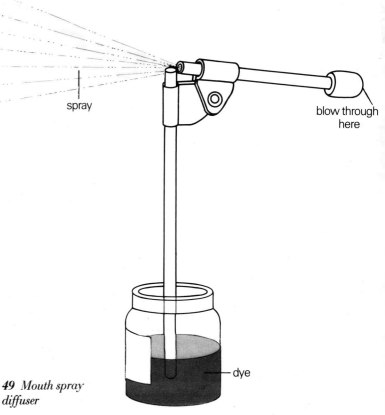

spray

blow through here

dye

49 Mouth spray diffuser

Three quilted cushion covers

half, along the length, with the seams inside. Press the fold in place. Run two rows of gathering stitches, about 1 cm (³⁄₈ in) in from the raw edge of the fabric, and then pull up the gathers to fit round your circle. Lay the frill on to the right side of the quilted fabric, match up the raw edges and pin in place, spreading out the gathers evenly to fit. Tack in place all round. Lay the backing fabric circle on top of this, right sides inside, and tack all round. Stitch around the edge, leaving a gap about 25 cm (10 in) open for turning the cover and inserting the cushion pad. As with the other cushions you could also insert a zip across the backing piece to insert the pad easily.

Remove all the tacking and gathering stitches and turn the cushion cover right sides out. Press very lightly, if necessary, and insert the cushion pad. Turn under the raw edges and slip stitch the gap to neaten.

subtle colours of your first spraying. Leave the quilting to dry completely in a warm place, still pinned out.

Using a large pair of compasses draw out a 38 cm (15 in) diameter circle on to paper and cut it out. Use this pattern to cut out one circle of silk for the cushion back, and the same sized circle from your piece of quilting. Zig-zag stitch all round the edge of the quilting, to neaten.

Cut two 10 cm (4 in) wide strips of silk, whose length extends the whole width of the fabric. Join the two pieces, right sides together, at the short edges to form a circle. Put this over the arm of your ironing board and fold it in

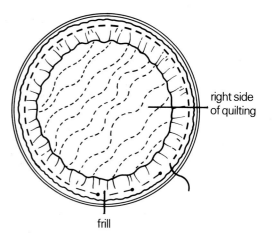

right side of quilting

frill

50 *Pin and tack the frill on to the right side of the cushion cover front*

9 PAINTED CUSHION

This circular cushion has a hand painted and quilted cover made in silk and finished with a frilled edge. The design is drawn very lightly on to the silk and then painted with fabric paints. When it is dry and the colours have been fixed, the fabric is then quilted, following the lines of the design. You can use a variety of stitches and coloured thread, hand or machine stitching and any combination of bead decoration and braids. Here is your chance to experiment and see what lovely results come up by accident, as well as design. This cushion is just one example of what can be done and gives you the basic directions and order of working. It is up to you to come up with your own version, as no two cushions will ever look quite the same.

MATERIALS

60 m (¾ yd) plain silk in white or cream
A 40 cm (16 in) square of 113 g (4 oz) terylene wadding
A 40 cm (16 in) square of calico or poplin backing fabric
Fabric paints and sable watercolour brushes
1 round cushion pad 38 cm (15 in) diameter
Clean white blotting paper
Various threads
Drawing pins, a pair of compasses and cartridge paper
Beads and braid to tone as desired
Pattern (see page 73)

MAKING UP

(1 cm (⅜ in) seam allowance throughout)
Draw out your design full size, on to white cartridge paper using a black waterproof felt pen. Place this on the work surface and pin or tape a 40 cm (16 in) square of the silk on top. Trace the design through very lightly, in pencil or embroidery felt pen. Now lay out some clean blotting paper and pin the fabric over it, on to your work surface. Mix up the fabric paints to the colours that you want following the manufacturer's instructions. Paint the design on to the fabric using the sable watercolour brushes. You can either leave the paint to dry before putting on the next colour, for a clearly defined effect, or else paint quickly and let the colours run into each other, for a softer, watery look. A combination of the two techniques will probably be best, but try experimenting on a spare piece of fabric. Leave the paint to dry with the fabric still pinned on the blotting paper. When dry, remove the pins and press the fabric following the manufacturer's instructions, in order to fix the dyes.

Now prepare the fabrics for quilting. Lay the calico square on your work surface wrong side up, then place the wadding on top. Lastly, place the painted silk on top of these, right side up. Match up the raw edges and tack through all the layers, across the centre and round the edge. Put the work on to the machine and start stitching near the centre of the fabric. Gradually work out towards the edge, with the stitching lines following the shape of the main design, rather like the contour lines on a map. Remember that rows of quilting close together will tend to flatten the fabrics, and rows stitched further apart will give a more quilted look. Use this in your work to help the design. Change the colour and type of stitching, to give added variety. When you have finished machine stitching, decide whether to add further detail. When you feel all the stitching is complete, remove the tacking and pin the fabric over damp blotting paper to stretch it back into shape (see page 23). Use a pair of compasses to draw out a 38 cm (15 in) circle on the cartridge paper, cut this out carefully. Pin the circle on to the quilted fabric and cut it out; also cut out a circle of plain silk for the back of the cushion. Zig-zag stitch all round the edge of the quilting, to neaten.

Now make the edging frill. Cut two 10 cm (4 in) wide strips of the plain silk, across the width of the fabric. Join the two pieces, at the short ends, with right sides together, to form a circle. Put this over the arm of your ironing board and fold it in half, along the length, with the seams inside. Press the fold in place. Make two rows of gathering stitches, about 1 cm (½ in), from the edge and pull up the gathers, to fit round the edge of the circle. Place the frill on to the right side of the quilted circle, match up the raw edges and pin in place, spreading out the gathering evenly. Tack all round. Lay the cushion back piece over this, right sides inside, and tack in place. Stitch all round, leaving a gap about 25 cm (10 in) open, for turning the cover and inserting the cushion pad. You could insert a zip in the cushion back, before cutting out and sewing it, to make it easier to insert the cushion pad.

Remove all the tacking and gathering stitches and turn the cover right sides out. Press carefully, if necessary, and insert the cushion pad through the gap in the stitching. Fold in the raw edges of fabric and slip stitch together.

10 COT QUILT

This is a quilt for a baby's cot featuring the puff quilting method. It is made using six different coloured fabrics in cotton lawn and voile. These usually come in delicate pastel shades and are ideal for a small baby. The finished size of the quilt is 75 cm × 95 cm (29½ in × 37½ in) which should fit an average-sized cot. This would also be an ideal method to use for cot bumpers to match the quilt.

MATERIALS
20 cm (¼ yd) of each of six different fabrics
1 m (1 yd) of a backing fabric to tone – this could be one of the puff patch fabrics – 115 cm (45 in) wide
1.20 m (1¼ yd) of 227 g (8 oz) wadding
Stiff card for templates
1 m (1¼ yd) of plain white or pale-coloured poplin for the backing squares for each patch.

MAKING UP
(5 mm (¼ in) seam unless otherwise stated)
Using a sharp knife and a set square, mark and cut out two templates from the stiff card. The first should measure 12 cm (4¾ in) square for the top fabrics and the other should measure 10 cm (4 in) square for the backing fabric. Iron your backing fabric and lay it out on your work surface. Using a sharp pencil, draw round the smaller template very accurately to make sixty-three squares. Cut out these carefully. Iron your top fabrics and draw round the larger template to make sixty-three squares altogether, in a mixture of the different fabrics. Take one top square and pin it to one backing square at the four corners. Have the right sides of the fabric outside and match up the corners carefully. Make a flat box pleat at the centre of each side of the square to take in the fullness of the top fabric. Pin the pleats in position on the backing fabric. Now stitch round three sides, either by hand or machine, removing the pins as you go. Tack the pleat on the fourth side in place, leaving that side open. Stitch all the top squares to the backing squares in the same way to make sixty-three tiny cushions.

Now cut 8 cm (3¼ in) wide strips of the wadding. Cut these into 8 cm (3¼ in) squares. Place two wadding squares together and insert them into one of the fabric cushions. Pin the open raw edges together and stitch

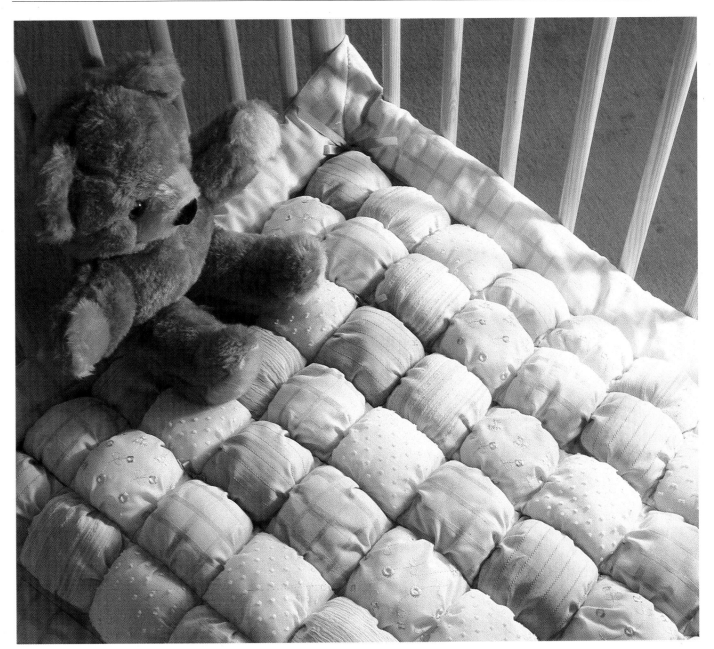

Cot quilt

across to hold the wadding inside. Repeat this with all the squares.

Lay the sixty-three cushions out on the work surface in seven rows of nine, rearranging the squares until you have a satisfactory pattern of squares, or a random mixture with no two similar fabrics next to each other. You may need to make up additional squares to achieve the desired effect.

Picking up the squares one by one, tack all the squares from one vertical row together. Keep the right sides of the top fabrics together and then stitch accurate 5 mm (¼ in) seams. Repeat this with all the rows and then press the seams flat on the reverse side, taking care not to squash the wadding too much. Now stitch these strips together, in the right order, with rights sides together and raw edges level. Make sure the seams of the squares match up accurately. This forms the padded centre of your quilt.

Lay out the piece of fabric for the back and the edge of the cot quilt on the work surface, with wrong sides uppermost. Lay the padded centre piece in the middle of this, right side uppermost and tack in place all round the edge. Trim the fabric so that it is exactly 18 cm (7 in) larger all round than the padded piece. Cut four 8 cm (3¼ in) wide strips of the wadding to fit round the edge of your quilt and tack them in place round the padded centre section. Trim the wadding square at the corners.

Now fold the backing fabric over the edge of the wadding, turn under a small hem and tack in place all round the edge of the centre piece, making sure all the raw edges are covered. At the corners, fold the fabric under to form a neat mitre. Trim away any lumpy excess

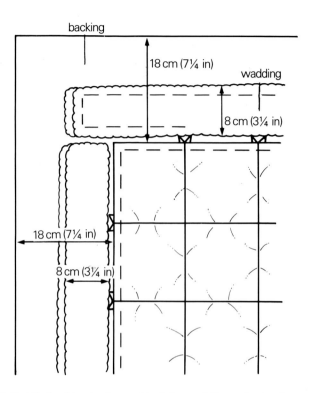

51 Cut the backing to size and tack the wadding strips in place

fabric if it becomes too bulky. Hand stitch the mitres neatly. Now hand or machine stitch all round the finish. You could stitch a piece of satin ribbon along the join finishing with a bow at each corner for a pretty effect. Make a few tie quilting stitches across the centre of the quilt, to hold the backing fabric to the padded section. Tie off at the back and add tiny bows of ribbon at each point on the front, if you like.

11 WINDOW BLIND

This is a semi-transparent window blind that looks just as good from both sides. It can be used with standard roller blind fixings and is most suitable for a smallish window. It features mainly shadow quilting with some cording and surface embroidery. It is based on two layers of fine net with different-coloured fabrics trapped between the layers and held in place with stitching. The fabrics should not be too thick or the blind will not go round the roller successfully. I have chosen a landscape design and there is a squared pattern for this but if you need to change dimensions for your window, you must adapt the design to fit. This technique could also be used to make a screen or lampshade.

MATERIALS

(For a window measuring 115 cm × 100 cm,
45 in × 39 in)
2.50 m (2¾ yd) of fine white nylon net, at least 120 cm
(48 in) wide
Various pieces of fine, non-fraying fabric in greens,
blues, yellows and browns
Coloured yarns
Embroidery thread
Cartridge paper and waterproof black felt pen
Tracing paper
Roller blind kit to fit window
Pattern (see page 78)

MAKING UP

Using white cartridge paper and a waterproof black felt pen, draw out the design to full size using a grid of squares. Use tracing paper, to trace off and cut out the individual shapes of the fields, hedges, etc. numbering them to help identify them later. Iron all the fabrics and pin the pattern pieces on to the appropriate fabrics.

Choose the colours following the design, assessing the depth of colour when held up to the light as well as the colour when it lies flat on the work surface.

Fold the net in half across the width and press. Place this fold 2.5 cm (1 in) below the lower edge line on your pattern. This will form the channel to hold the batten along the lower edge of the blind. Pin or tape this edge of the net over the pattern and then lift back the top layer of net. Now pin or tape all round the edge of the net to hold it in position over the pattern. Unpin the patterns from the fabric shapes one by one and lay them on to the net background. Tack them in place. Use the numbering system to get them all in the correct place. Butt the edges of the fabric together so there are no gaps to let the light through, unless you are leaving a cording channel.

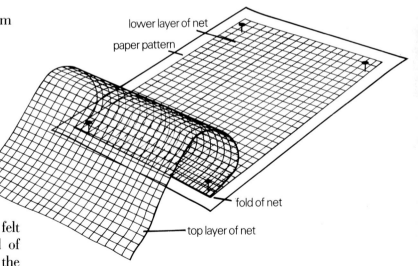

lower layer of net

paper pattern

fold of net

top layer of net

52 Pin lower layer of net over pattern and lift back top layer

53

Window blind

Carefully fold over the top layer of net to enclose the fabric pieces, and tack in place across the centre and round the edge so that there will be no slipping.

The next stage is to stitch all round each area. Start stitching the sky areas first and then work downwards towards the foreground. For areas next to a cording channel, use straight machine stitch but for butting, you can use a machine zig-zag stitch or satin stitch, depending on the effect you want. Choose thread colours to blend with the fabrics on, or near, the horizon and contrasting or brighter shades for areas nearer the foreground. You can use hand stitching instead of machine stitching but remember it will be seen on both sides, so a neat running stitch is best.

When you have completed the outline stitching, thread coloured yarn through the channels to represent hedges and fences. There is no need to cut the net, just push the needle or bodkin holding the yarn through the holes in the net. Stitch lines of embroidery and looped areas of yarn by hand.

Now machine stitch the channel in the lower edge of the blind. Measure and cut the roller to the corrrect length for the window, following the manufacturer's instructions. Carefully measure the finished width of your blind and use a pencil to mark the net on both sides making sure the marks are at right angles to the lower edge. This is most important as the blind will not roll up evenly and straight if this is not accurate. The finished width of the blind should be about 2 cm (¾ in) narrower than the roller. Cut along the pencil lines and then zig-zag stitch the layers together, changing the thread colours where necessary to make the stitching as unobtrusive as possible.

Mark a pencil line along the wooden roller and another line across the top of your blind about 2.5 cm (1 in) from the top edge. Once again, this must be at exact right angles to the sides. Attach the blind to the roller using tacks or a staple gun, matching up the two pencil lines. Leave an equal gap at each end of the roller. Insert the batten in the channel at the lower edge of the blind – you may need to paint the roller and the batten first to blend in with your design. Put up the roller blind in the window recess following the manufacturer's instructions. Screw cord to the centre of the batten.

12 GIRL'S PINAFORE DRESS

This is a two-colour pinafore dress, made in polycotton poplin, to fit a girl aged seven to eight years old. The bodice, at the front and back, is lightly padded and features tied quilting. A very narrow satin ribbon, tied in tiny bows on the right side of the fabric, provides added decoration. The back fastens with a zip and the skirt has bands of satin ribbon stitched on to the fabric and then padded with quilting wool, to give it body. The dress looks very pretty with a fancy blouse worn underneath, or on its own as a lovely, summer party dress.

MATERIALS

1.5 m (1¾ yd) of grey polycotton poplin 115 cm (45 in) wide

40 cm (½ yd) of red polycotton poplin 115 cm (45 in) wide

5.20 m (5¾ yd) of grey satin ribbon 1.5 mm (¹⁄₁₆ in) wide

Satin ribbon (single face) in varying widths and colours of red, white and grey. You will need at least 2.5 m (3 yd) of each ribbon

A 45 cm (18 in) zip
Quilting wool and yarn needle or bodkin
Dressmakers' graph paper and a pencil
20 cm (¼ yd) of 113 g (4 oz) terylene wadding
Threads to match fabric and ribbons
Pattern (see pages 76–77)

MAKING UP

(1.5 cm (⅝ in) seam allowance throughout)
Draw out the pattern to full size using graph paper and a pencil. Cut out the shapes along the outlines. Pin the front bodice on to a double piece of the red fabric and cut out, adding 2 cm (¾ in) all round the outside to allow for quilting. Mark through the paper with a sharp pencil at the tied quilting points. Mark the top fabric only. Cut out two pairs of back bodice pieces in the same way, allowing 2 cm (¾ in) extra all round and marking the tied quilting points on the top layer of fabric. Unpin these pattern pieces and use them to cut one front bodice and a pair of back bodice pieces from 113 g (4 oz) terylene wadding, again adding 2 cm (¾ in) all round the edges. Place the wadding piece between the two pieces of the front bodice with the right sides of the fabric outside. Tack them together, across the centre and round the edge.

Thread a yarn needle with very narrow grey satin ribbon and, starting on the right side, put the needle through all the layers of fabric at one of the central marked points. Bring the needle out at the front of the work, a little way away and then repeat this stitch, in the same holes, finishing at the front of the work. Leave long ends of ribbon and tie these into a tiny bow. Cut off the ends neatly and do not waste too much ribbon. You should leave about 8 cm (3 in) of ribbon free after the first stitch. Working out towards the edge of the fabric make tiny bows, in the same way, at all the marked points on the front bodice. Tie the bows so that they all face the same way and are of a uniform size. Repeat this

process with the two back bodice pieces after placing the wadding between the fabric layers and tacking in place. Now pin the bodice pattern pieces back on to the quilted fabric. Match up the tied quilting points and then cut the pieces out accurately, on the outlines.

Pin on the pattern and cut out the shoulder and side pieces from the grey fabric. Remove the pattern from the fabric and pin the shoulder pieces together in pairs, with right sides inside. Stitch down the long edges along the seam line. Turn the shoulder pieces right sides out and press. Make a line of top-stitching along each fold about 5 mm (¼ in) from the edge. Lay bands of satin ribbon on to the right side of one shoulder piece and pin in place when you are happy with the arrangement. Stitch the ribbons in place, close to their edges, with matching thread. Thread a yarn needle with quilting wool and pad the channels directly behind the ribbons. Do not make them too stiff or the shoulder pieces will not sit properly. Make the other shoulder piece to match the first one.

Fold the two side pieces in half, along the marked line, with right sides outside. Press and make a row of top stitching on each, 5 mm (¼ in) from the fold. Now, with right sides together, pin and tack the shoulder pieces and the side pieces to the front bodice. Stitch in place on the bodice front along the seam line, going through the top fabric and the wadding only and leaving the lining free. Trim the wadding close to the stitching and along the seam line on the bodice top and sides. Open out the shoulder and side pieces and then turn under the top fabric on these three sides of the bodice. Turn in the lining on the same three sides and slip stitch in place to cover the wadding and enclose the raw edges.

Now stitch the other ends of the shoulder pieces and side pieces to the back bodice pieces, in the same way. Finish as for front bodice, leaving the lower edge and the centre back edges open.

Next, cut out the skirt fabric from the grey poplin.

Girl's pinafore dress

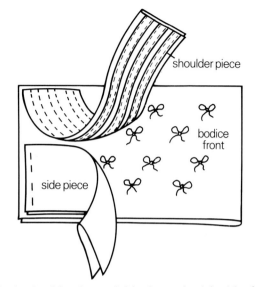

53 *Pin the shoulder piece and side piece to the right side of your bodice*

This measures 65 cm × 150 cm (25½ in × 59 in). Press it flat and lay it out on your work surface. Place several pieces of the satin ribbon across the fabric, about 15 cm (6 in) away from one long, raw edge. This is the hem edge. Work upwards from this, with several bands of ribbon, in varying widths and colours. Make sure they run parallel to the raw edge, finalize your arrangement and then tack in place. Top stitch the ribbons, using matching thread and sewing very close to the edges of the ribbon. Remove the tacking stitches.

Thread a yarn needle or bodkin with a long piece of quilting wool and pad the channels behind the wider ribbons. Do not make it too stiff; one or two strands will be sufficient. Trim off the ends of the quilting wool level with the fabric. Now, with the right sides together, pin the two short ends of the skirt piece together, to form the centre back seam. Stitch up from the hem edge to a point 26 cm (10 in) away from the top edge. Press the seam open on the reverse side of the fabric.

Run two rows of gathering stitches either side of the seam line along the top edge of the skirt. Pull up the gathers until the skirt fits the lower edge of the bodice. Pin and tack the skirt to the bodice, with right sides facing and matching up the centre back raw edges. Open out the layers of the bodice fabric so that you stitch the skirt to the wadding and the top fabrics only. Trim the wadding close to the stitching line. Remove the gathering and tacking stitches. Now turn under the backing fabric on the bodice and slip stitch in place along the seam line, to enclose all the raw edges and wadding.

Top stitch bands of ribbon round the edge of the padded pieces to decorate. Pin and tack them in place first, folding the ribbon under at the corners, to form tiny mitres.

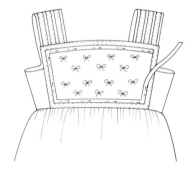

54 *Pin and stitch bands of ribbon round the edges of the padded bodice*

Tack the zip in place, down the centre back. Stitch it to the top fabrics and wadding only. Trim away the surplus wadding from the seam and then fold the backing fabric under and slip stitch to the reverse of the zip to hide all the raw edges.

Try the pinafore dress on the child and pin up the hem to the correct length. Turn and press under a 5 mm (¼ in) hem along the raw edge. Then tack and slip stitch the hem neatly to finish.

13 THE PATCHWORK QUILT

This quilt fits a double bed measuring approximately 245 cm (96½ in) square. It is made in the simplest and quickest form of patchwork which is machine sewn squares. It uses twelve different fabrics in one basic colour, blue, ranging in tone from light to dark. You can machine or hand quilt the patchwork to make up the padded quilt. The design is based on the Amish 'Sunshine and Shadow' quilts, with the square patches arranged in a diamond formation. You can adjust the size of the quilt to fit your bed exactly, by adding or subtracting squares to the pattern or changing the width of the border. If you do this, always keep an odd number of squares in each direction, or the pattern will not work.

MATERIALS
1.5 m (1½ yd) of twelve different Liberty Tana Lawn fabrics, in toning and contrasting colours and patterns ranging from pale to dark
8.10 m (9 yd) of plain Tana Lawn for a backing fabric and to form the border. Choose a toning colour
8.10 m (9 yd) of 113 g (4 oz) terylene wadding
Cottons to match the basic colour of the quilt
Stiff card or acetate to make templates (or manufactured 8 cm (3 in) square template)
Set square, ruler and craft knife
Squared paper and felt pens to work out the design
Small polythene bags for storing ready cut fabric squares
Pattern (see page 79)

MAKING UP
(1 cm (⅜ in) seam allowance throughout)
Cut out an 8 cm (3⅛ in) square very accurately from stiff card or acetate using a set square and craft knife. If you are using stiff card, cut several templates the same as the edges will get worn from use. Use this template to mark out squares of the fabrics. Place the template on the reverse of your fabric after ironing. Draw round it with a sharp pencil, an embroidery felt pen or a chalk pencil. Cut out quite a number of squares from each fabric. Lay these squares out on a large table and arrange the various colours in a design following the diagram. When you have decided the order in which to place each fabric, mark this on to squared paper and number each fabric. Cut out scraps of each fabric and staple them to a piece of card with numbers alongside for a key. Take the central, horizontal row of squares in the quilt and pin all these squares in the correct order with right sides together. Stitch them together with a straight machine stitch, tacking accurate 1 cm (⅜ in) seams and removing the pins as you sew. It is important to be really accurate at this stage, so that the seam lines of the squares line up exactly when you sew the rows together. If necessary, draw a pencil line on the base plate of your sewing machine exactly 1 cm (⅜ in) from the needle to help keep the seams accurate, or use a strip of masking tape.

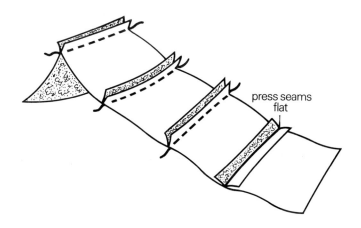

press seams flat

55 Pin the squares together, right sides facing, and stitch

Patchwork quilt

Continue making up the remaining horizontal rows in this way, ticking off each row on your diagram when you have stitched it. Draw a tiny reference number on a small self adhesive label and put it on the end of each row of squares for identification later. Mark and cut out more squares from all the fabrics as you need them. Keep them in small, numbered polythene bags until they are to be used.

When you have stitched all the squares into horizontal rows, press open all the seams flat, on the reverse side. Now lay out the strips in order and pin them together, right sides facing, to form the quilt. Make sure the seam lines of the squares match up. Stitch all the strips together, taking 1 cm (⅜ in) seams. Press open all the seams on the reverse side of the patchwork.

Cut the backing fabric into three 2.70 m (106 in) lengths and stitch them along the selvedges, taking a 1 cm (⅜ in) seam and keeping right sides together. Press the seams open.

Cut the terylene wadding into three 2.70 m (106 in) lengths and butt the long edges together to form one large piece. Ladder stitch or oversew by hand on both sides of the wadding along both joins.

Patchwork quilt (detail)

If you are going to hand stitch the layers of the quilt, mount the backing fabric into a frame and then tack the wadding and patchwork centrally on top (page 31).

If you are going to machine stitch the quilt, lay the backing out on a large work surface or on the floor, wrong side up, then the wadding, and finally position the patchwork centrally. All the right sides of the fabric should be facing outside. It is important that all the fabrics are flat at this stage. Tack all over carefully, through all the layers, across the centre and round the edge (page 22). Now stitch the quilt with a straight stitch on the machine or a running stitch by hand. Choose a thread colour to blend with most of the fabrics. You can follow the straight lines of the squares for your stitching, quilting along the seam of every other row in both

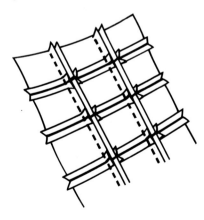

56 Pin and stitch the strips together, right sides facing

directions. You could also stitch diagonally from corner to corner on the squares. This will help to accentuate the diamond design of the colour groupings. Once again quilt every other row. Also make a line of stitching 1 cm (⅜ in) in from the raw edge of the patchwork, all round the edge.

When you have completed all the stitching, remove the tacking stitches and trim the wadding, only, to 10.5 cm (4 in) outside the edge of the patchwork. Trim the backing fabric 12.5 cm (5 in) outside this. Fold over and press a 1 cm (⅜ in) hem to the wrong side. Bring the backing fabric over the wadding and pin it to the front of the patchwork up to the line of stitching, to completely cover all the raw edges and the wadding. Fold under the corners of the fabric into neat mitres. Trim away any surplus fabric that will not lie flat at the corners. Pin and then hand stitch the mitres in place. Hand stitch the border in place, on to the patchwork, all round the edge.

57 Trim backing to size, press hem and fold over mitres

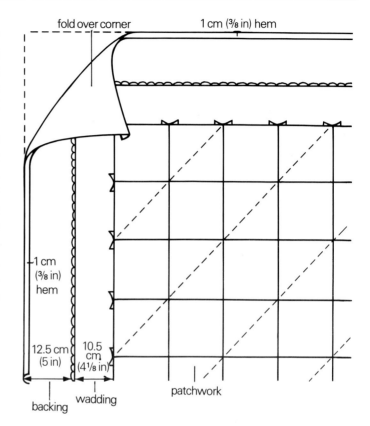

14 TABLE OF FABRICS FOR QUILTING

ENGLISH OR WADDED QUILTING

Top fabric Light-weight silks, jersey, wool/cotton mixtures, thin suede or leather, satin, cotton, lawn, fine wool, dress fabric, brushed nylon, velour, towelling, velvet, taffeta, wild silk, calico, crêpe, denim, poplin, needlecord, polycotton

Wadding Terylene wadding 57 g (2 oz), 113 g (4 oz) and 227 g (8 oz). Flannelette, domette, blanket, cotton wadding

Backing fabric Same as top fabric for a reversible effect, also muslin, sheeting, curtain lining, synthetic dress linings.

PAINTED QUILTING

Top fabric Plain silk, calico, lawn, poplin, satin, jersey

Wadding As for English, trapunto or Italian quilting depending on technique used

Backing fabric As for English, trapunto or Italian quilting, depending on technique used

PATTERNED QUILTING

Top fabric Any patterned dress cottons, lawn, voile, gingham, light-weight upholstery fabric, silk, wool, jersey, wool/cotton mixtures

Wadding As for English, trapunto or Italian quilting, depending on technique used

Backing fabric As for English, trapunto or Italian quilting, depending on technique used

SPRAYED QUILTING

Top fabric Plain silks, calico, lawn, poplin, satin, jersey

Wadding As for English, trapunto or Italian quilting, depending on technique used

Backing As for English, trapunto or Italian quilting depending on technique used

RANDOM QUILTING

Top fabric As for English quilting in plain colours or previously sprayed or painted

Wadding As for English quilting

Backing fabric As for English quilting

TRAPUNTO QUILTING

Top fabric Jersey, crêpe, velour, silk, cotton, wool/cotton mixtures, thin suede or leather, lawn

Wadding Scraps of synthetic wadding, sheeps' wool, kapok

Backing fabric Muslin, calico, lawn, poplin, sheeting

SHADOW QUILTING

Top fabric Organdie, organza, chiffon, georgette, net

Wadding Brightly-coloured silk, felt or wool

Backing fabric Same as top fabric for a reversible see-through effect, or the same as for English quilting (remember the backing colour will show through on the right side of the work)

ITALIAN QUILTING

Top fabric Jersey, crêpe, silk, wool/cotton mixtures, fine linen, poplin, fine suede or leather, ribbon

Wadding Quilting wool, or similar loosely-spun knitting wool, cord

Backing fabric Good-quality muslin, linen scrim, calico

FLAT QUILTING

Top fabric Felt, wool, needlecord, linen, satin, calico, taffeta, poplin, velvet, silk, denim

Wadding No wadding

Backing fabric As for English quilting and felt

continued

APPLIQUÉ QUILTING

Top fabric Lawn, poplin, dress fabric, silk, wool/cotton mixtures

Wadding As for English or trapunto quilting, depending on the technique used

Backing fabric As for English quilting

TIED QUILTING

Top fabric Silk, cotton, lawn, voile, fine wool, poplin

Wadding Domette, flannelette, terylene wadding

Backing fabric As for English quilting

PUFF QUILTING

Top fabric Silk, lawn, wool/cotton mixtures, cotton, poplin, voile, fine wool

Wadding Terylene wadding, scraps of synthetic wadding, sheeps' wool

Backing fabric Calico, poplin, lawn, sheeting, muslin

GLOSSARY

FABRICS

Top layer This is the top layer of fabric on your work and the 'right side', that will be on view when the work is complete.

Wadding This is the padding that gives the quilting its three-dimensional quality. It can be a variety of materials, like terylene or polyester wadding, felt, domette, kapok or quilting wool depending on the type of quilting.

Backing This describes the fabric that covers the back of the quilting which is present in all quilting except the one layer Italian quilting method. It is usually a special fabric like calico, muslin or poplin but it can be the same, or similar, to the top fabric, when used for reversible work and on clothing.

HAND STITCHING

Tacking This is the same as running stitch but the stitches should be larger. It is used for the temporary joining of layers of fabric prior to quilting, to stop the fabrics from slipping and it is also used to attach the appliqué shapes.

Oversewing This is useful for sewing the raw edges together on the backing fabric in trapunto quilting, and for joining wadding and fabrics where they will not be seen.

Ladder stitch This is a simple stitch that should be virtually invisible when complete. It is used for drawing up the cut edges after trapunto quilting and for joining two butted edges of wadding to form a larger piece.

Slip stitch This is a very neat, almost invisible stitch used for hems and for stitching the openings on cushion covers and finishing bindings. You should aim for a small stitch, joining the two layers and a longer stitch slipping under the fabric and hidden from view.

Herring-bone stitch This is used for stitching the cord in place on the one-layer Italian quilting method. It can also be used for joining the edges of wadding.

EMBROIDERY STITCHES

Blanket stitch This is very useful along an edge and for attaching appliquéd shapes to your work. It gives a neat finish, preventing a certain amount of fraying and can be worked in a matching or contrasting colour. Keep the stitches fairly small and regularly spaced. If stitched very close together, you produce a buttonhole stitch which prevents raw edges from any fraying.

Satin stitch When done by hand this produces lovely smooth 'cushions' of embroidery, very effective for flower centres, small leaves and initials. It is best for surface embroidery on small areas.

Stem stitch This can be useful for lines of quilting or for decorative surface embroidery. It produces a smooth line, suitable for outlining shapes and for the veins in leaves, stems or stamens. It is not suitable for quilting on reversible work.

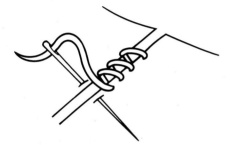

58 *Oversewing*

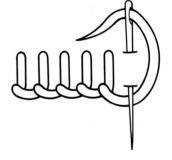

61 *Blanket stitch*

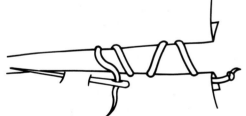

59 *Ladder stitch*

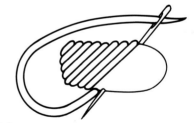

62 *Satin stitch*

60 *Slip stitch*

63 *Stem stitch*

BOOK LIST

Colby, Averil, *Quilting* (BT Batsford, 1972)

Brown, Elsa, *Creative Quilting* (Pitman, 1975)

Fitzrandolph, Mavis and Fletcher, Florence, *Quilting Traditional Methods and Design* (Reeves Dryad Press, 1972)

Hinson, Dolores A., *Quilting Manual* (Dover Publications, 1970)

James, Michael, *The Quiltmaker's Handbook* and *The Second Quiltmaker's Handbook* (Prentice-Hall Inc)

Johnson, Georgette, *Quilting* (Search Press, 1978)

McMorris, Penny, *Quilting – An Introduction to American Patchwork Design* (BBC Publications, 1984)

McNeill, Moyra, *Quilting* (Octopus Books, 1980)

Meyer, Franz Sales, *Handbook of Ornament* (Dover Publications, 1957)

Mirow, Gregory, *A Treasury of Design for Artists and Craftsmen* (Dover Publications, 1969)

Short, Eirian, *Quilting – Technique, Design and Application* (BT Batsford, 1979)

Walker, Michele, *Good Housekeeping: Quilting and Patchwork* (Ebury Press, 1983)

PATTERNS

Design for trapunto quilting, each square represents 2 cm (³/₄ in)

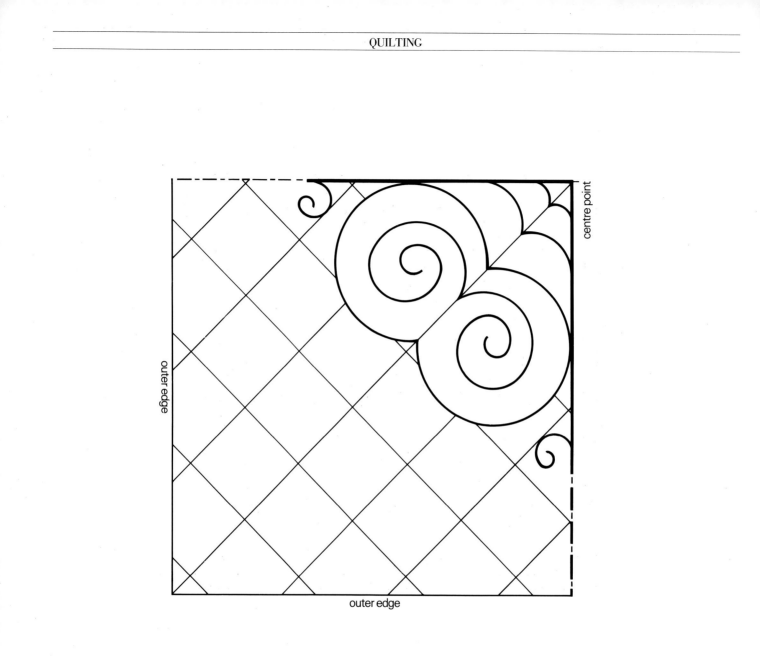

A quarter of the repeating design for English quilting

A quarter of the repeating design for Italian quilting

Design for flat quilting, each square equals 2 cm (3/4 in). Shaded areas are to be cut out after stitching.

top

Design for painted quilting, each square equals 2 cm (³/₄ in)

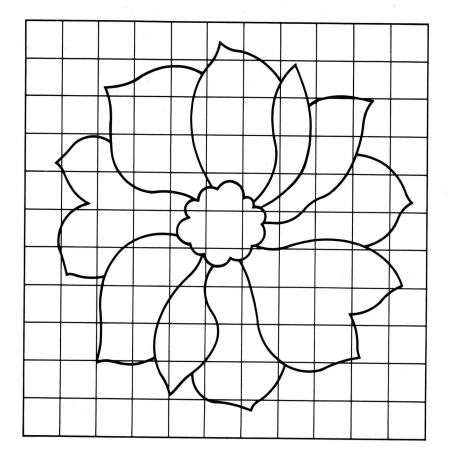

Design for appliqué quilting each square represents 2 cm (³/₄ in)

Design for painted cushion, each square represents 2 cm (³/₄ in)

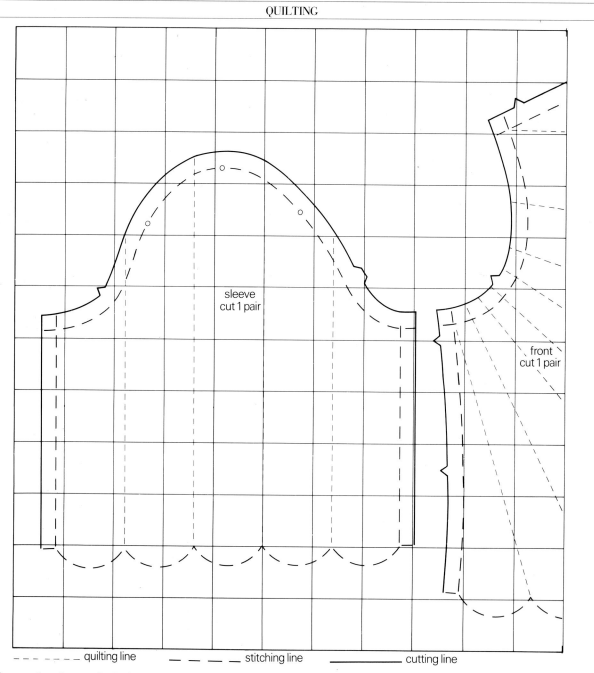

sleeve
cut 1 pair

front
cut 1 pair

– – – – – – quilting line   – – – – – stitching line   ———— cutting line

Above and opposite *Pattern for jacket size 12 / 14, each square represents 5 cm (2 in)*

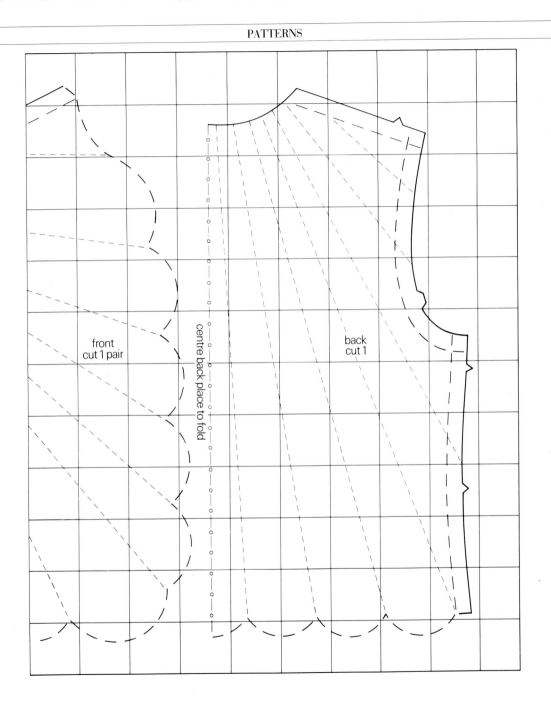

front
cut 1 pair

centre back place to fold

back
cut 1

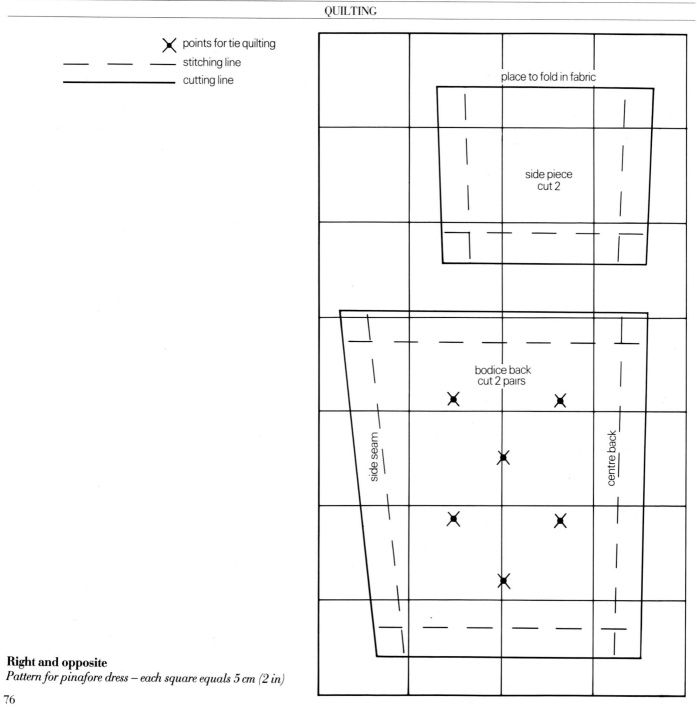

X points for tie quilting
— — — stitching line
—————— cutting line

place to fold in fabric

side piece
cut 2

bodice back
cut 2 pairs

side seam

centre back

Right and opposite
Pattern for pinafore dress – each square equals 5 cm (2 in)

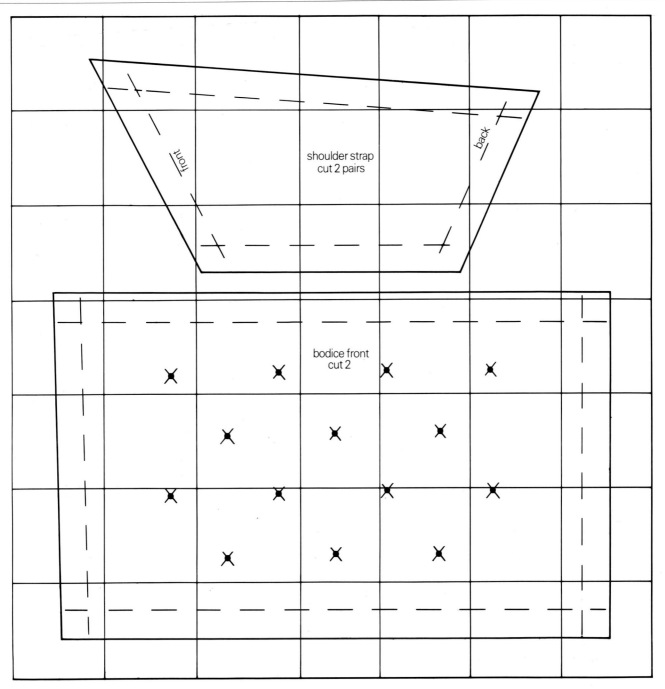

shoulder strap
cut 2 pairs

front

back

bodice front
cut 2

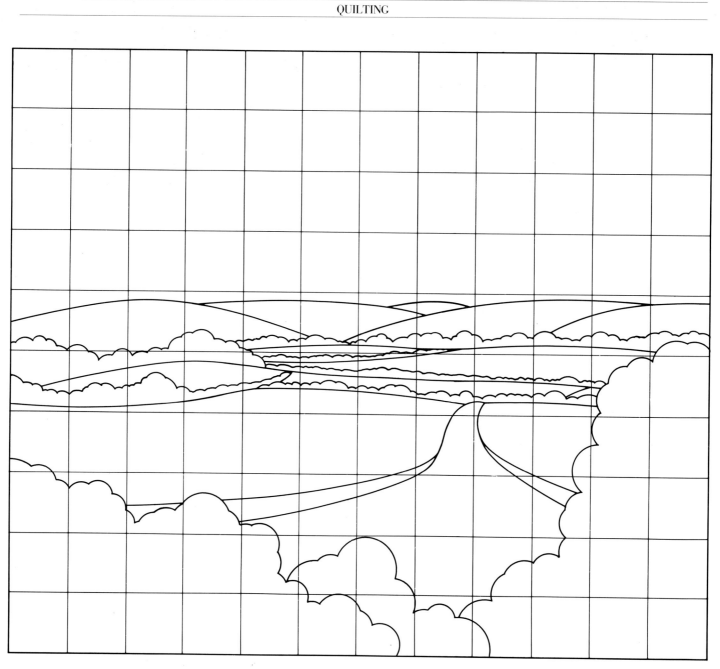

Design for window blind, each square equals 10 cm (4 in)

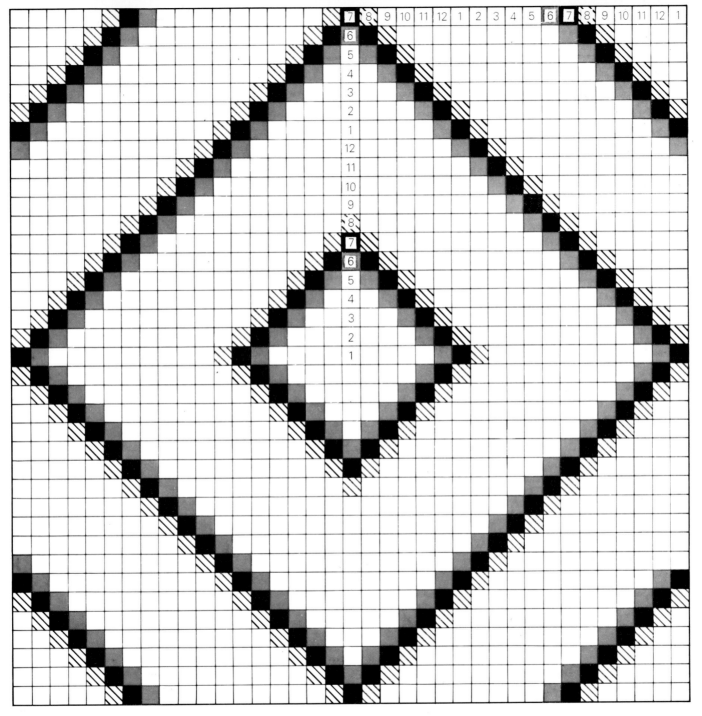

INDEX